My God

ᔃ · ᔄ

Letters from the famous
on God and the life hereafter

Collected and edited by
Hayley Mills and Marcus Maclaine

PELHAM BOOKS

*This book is dedicated to all
God's children*

PELHAM BOOKS

Published by the Penguin Group
27 Wrights Lane, London W8 5TZ, England
Viking Penguin Inc., 40 West 23rd Street, New York, New York 10010, USA
Penguin Books Australia Ltd, Ringwood, Victoria, Australia
Penguin Books Canada Ltd, 2801 John Street, Markham, Ontario, Canada L3R 1B4
Penguin Books (NZ) Ltd, 182–190 Wairau Road, Auckland 10, New Zealand

Penguin Books Ltd, Registered Offices: Harmondsworth, Middlesex, England

First published 1988

Printed and bound in Great Britain by Butler & Tanner Ltd, Frome
Typeset by Wilmaset in 11/12pt Ehrhardt

A CIP catalogue record for this book is available from the British Library
ISBN 0 7207 1813 9

WHO OR WHAT IS YOUR PERSONAL CONCEPT OF GOD?

❧ · ☙

WHAT DO YOU BELIEVE HAPPENS TO YOU WHEN YOU DIE?

જે · ૬

GOD IS MORE TRULY IMAGINED THAN EXPRESSED,
AND HE EXISTS MORE TRULY THAN HE IS IMAGINED.

St Augustine

 જે · ૬

THE EVENT OF DEATH IS ALWAYS ASTOUNDING;
OUR PHILOSOPHY NEVER REACHES, NEVER POSSESSES IT;
WE ARE ALWAYS AT THE BEGINNING OF OUR CATECHISM;
ALWAYS THE DEFINITION IS YET TO BE MADE.
WHAT IS DEATH?

Ralph Waldo Emerson

 જે · ૬

Contents

◆§ · §◆

Illustrations

❧ · ❧

BUCKINGHAM PALACE

"The child must be protected beyond and above all considerations of race, nationality or creed". This is the first of the Rights of the Child drafted by our founder, Eglantyne Jebb, influenced by her own Christian upbringing, over 60 years ago - and it is the cornerstone of Save the Children's philosophy to this day. So it is particularly appropriate that the royalties from this book, which brings together concepts of God from so many of the world's great religions - should be going to support SCF's work.

Save the Children is committed to helping countries and communities to provide the food, health, care and hope that should be every child's birthright. Projects include immunisation, training for local health workers, help for the handicapped, clean water schemes, pre-school education and work with street children.

SCF has over 100 projects in the UK, where work is concentrated in the inner cities. As well as self-help family centres, there are schemes for unemployed youngsters, work with disabled and gypsy children and programmes to help under-fives get off to a good start in life.

Public support is vital if this work is to continue and I am delighted that this thought-provoking book will be helping to generate funds for children in need.

Anne

H.R.H. The Princess Royal
President of the Save the Children Fund

Preface

The idea behind this book was born out of a desire to know and to understand how people from different walks of life conceive of God and what they believe happens to them when they die.

We wanted to ask as wide a cross-section of people as possible: religious leaders and scientists, philosophers and politicians, explorers, people in the arts and public life. The response was overwhelming and as the book developed it appeared there were almost as many different ways of perceiving God as there are people, though in many cases a common thread could be seen running through them. Compiling this book has been an illuminating experience and has helped us to see much that unites us. We are all children upon this Earth sharing a common humanity and ultimate fate; even so we often find it hard to understand and be tolerant towards each other.

Hopefully in some small way this book will help bring about a better understanding of others' beliefs. Collecting all these letters turned out to be a far greater task than originally envisaged but one not to have been missed; it has been an inspiring and rewarding experience.

Our heartfelt gratitude to all those who contributed. Unfortunately, not all the letters we received could appear in this one volume and we would like to offer our thanks and sincere apologies to those who did respond but have not been included. The good will and generosity of all those who took the time in the midst of their busy lives to answer these two fundamental, though not easy, questions was magnificent.

It has been a rare privilege to be given a glimpse into another's heart and a lesson in human nature and the great goodness to be found there.

HAYLEY MILLS
MARCUS MACLAINE
April 1988

Sir Yehudi Menuhin OM, KBE

Who or what is your personal concept of God?

For me, God is a great circle ◯ all-encompassing, infinite and eternal in its ever-changing myriad parts, yet all related in motion; containing what we are and what we make of our lives and of our future life; full, yet empty; symbolic, yet real; spirit and flesh combined; conscious yet immutable; present yet distant; participating yet non-interfering; neither cruel nor compassionate.

What do you believe happens to you when you die?

Return to, or remain in the circle.
My faith is that every particle of man, organic or inorganic, is possessed of aspiration, love and understanding and that in the end love and wisdom are one.

John Cleese
Writer and actor

I have no concept of God, but I am content with this. My superficial reading about atomic physics indicates that our minds, conditioned by the ordinary world of three dimensions, simply cannot grasp the reality of the structure of matter. That being the case, it seems to me quite absurd to think that our minds could even begin to grasp the spiritual reality.

Nevertheless, I think we may be able to receive something

from the spiritual force in the universe if only we prepare ourselves to do so.

I suspect that when we die, the essential part of us returns to its source. I don't think this part will have much to do with our normal personalities though, which are largely shaped by various aspects of our egotism.

I hope this doesn't seem too oracular.

Cory Aquino
President of the Philippines

I look up to God as a creator of the universe and beyond, as my Father, Lord and Redeemer from whose presence I had come and to whom I will return after an interlude on earth. I consider Him as the fountain of all love, mercy and good on earth; that He guides the destinies of men and nations, and that we have to pray for His power and grace.

I am a devout Catholic and I believe in the after life. As our creed says, 'I believe in the resurrection of the body, and life everlasting . . .'
I believe there is a heaven, and I believe that if I die a good Christian, I will see my Creator face-to-face.

There is a native, elemental homing instinct in our souls which turns us to God as naturally as the flower turns to the sun.
Rufus M. Jones

Benazir Bhutto
Leader of the Pakistan People's Party

◄§ · ïë►

The concept of God in the three mono-theistic religions is not very different. There are fundamental similarities and only superficial differences. But, the concept of God is much more ancient than our modern religions. In *The Golden Bough*, Frazer traces this to primitive man, several hundred thousand years before Judaism. Their concept was based on the theory of cause and effect. The poly-theistic belief system of the primitive people conceptualized God as a powerful person, not very different from human beings, with the same desires and aptitudes. Someone who would reward when happy and destroy when unhappy. Hence to appease this god, sacrifices, religious rites, rituals and presentations of gifts were devised. Over a period of many thousand years these practices were institutionalized and priests, temples and ancient mythological stories sprang up.

Homer's *Odyssey* is entirely devoted to how gods lived, fought, conspired and took revenge on each other. A more advanced stage was reached in the Egypt of the Pharaohs, where kings became gods. One of them, Amon Re, declared himself the only god and called himself the Sun God. He did this to check the intrigues of the priests and their growing power. This was the first example of monotheism in the ancient society.

With sustained development of society, the needs of individuals and communities changed. Their dependence on natural phenomena was reduced. Man's consciousness, his awareness and his relentless struggle to control nature brought new ideas. He lost interest in primitive magical thinking and came to be in a better position to interpret some of these phenomena.

The stage was now set for a breakthrough in the spiritual and religious life of the people. Everywhere, whether it was Egypt of the Pharaohs, the Eastern Empire of the Romans, or the slave-infested tribal society of heartland Arabia, it was the same theme. Man has no right to oppress another man, as there is one God and all men are created equal. It is this egalitarian concept of mono-theistic religion which created a revolution in man's thinking. This is most pronounced in the case of Islam and is the principal reason for its rapid spread and acceptance.

In recent times, the Catholic Church has also responded to this challenge. Since the second Vatican held in the early sixties, the entire approach of the Church has tilted towards protecting socio-economic and political rights of the vast numbers of people living under dictatorships. This new attitude of the Church has contributed positively towards the emancipation of the people from dictatorship and has helped development of egalitarian and democratic societies.

It is impossible to separate the concept of God from religious beliefs in modern times. My belief in Islam and its message of egalitarianism and human dignity is inextricably linked with my belief in one God.

As for your second question, whether there is life after death and existence of heaven and hell, I can only say that everyone wants to play a second innings. The concept of heaven and hell must remain a matter of belief. It is not possible for me to speculate on this subject or provide an intellectual analysis.

Dr H. J. *Eysenck*

Professor of Psychology

It will be obvious to any intelligent observer that people differ very much in their religious attitudes, some believing strongly, others adopting atheistic views. There is now strong evidence from studies of twins that such attitudes are largely based on heredity; genetic factors account for well over half of all the influences which determine our religious beliefs. Although my father was nominally Catholic, my mother nominally Protestant, neither had any interest in religion, nor any belief in God, and my own views have always been strongly atheistic. My disbelief in the existence of God has been based on two major arguments. In the first place, as a scientist, I require proof for any assertion, and no such proof for the existence of God has been forthcoming. In the second place, there is a logical inconsistency between a belief in an all-powerful, all-merciful God, and the existence of evil in the world. I know the arguments by means of which adherents of religion attempt to get round this problem, but they are illogical, and do not hold water. St Augustine might say: 'Credo quia impossibile!', but I find it difficult to believe because it is impossible!

As regards my belief as to what happens when I die, the answer is very simple – I will cease to exist! It would be nice to believe in a future in which the wicked are punished, and the good rewarded, but I know of no evidence for such a wonderful future. Different religions, of course, have different heavens; personally I would prefer a future life in the company of Islamic Houris, rather than of cymbal-bashing and harp-playing Christian angels, but neither seems to me a likely proposition.

Pete Townshend
Musician

◄§ · §♦

Is there a God, an after-life? I don't know. I don't believe anyone knows. I don't think it matters whether they know. But life appears to be so mysterious and unfair that faith takes on unreasonable importance.

What we accept as state-of-the-art today can be completely superseded tomorrow. The mysteries of cancer, M.S. and sickle cell anaemia confound us today, but soon they will be unravelled and beaten. So it is with precarious religious faith. We most often base such faith on what we cannot understand. We look for hope because of our ignorance. That has always seemed sad to me, and one of the reasons religion has become a dirty word. People's ignorance is used to subjugate society.

I know I don't have the precise logic of C. S. Lewis but I try to base my faith on what I *can* understand. In my perception of both the good and the bad things in the world I come to feel enormously uplifted or dejected to the point where I feel almost god-like myself. Everything I feel tells me that experience is an eternal explosion limited only by the size of my heart and mind and the alertness of what I call my soul. Preposterous to set myself up as feeling any trace of God's presence, yet I do. I feel it in myself. Now I know it isn't *me* – I'm just about evolved far enough to stop myself breaking up perfectly innocent furniture – so it must be something, or *someone*, else.

If we were meant to have proof we would have it. I don't think we are meant to know, it just isn't part of nature's cycle. What is important is that we don't make what we *want* too important, but value what we already have. Now all this wisdom from someone who has only seen Holiday Inn motel rooms and dressing rooms for twenty-five years indicates to me that I stand a pretty good chance of having learned all this before I was even born. So I've more or less conclusively proved (to myself at least) that there is a God, and that I have been conscious in some way before this life.

Malcolm Muggeridge

My personal concept of God is that He is eternal and His Word is the source of all Love, Holiness, Truth, and Wisdom. As an unknown monk many centuries ago remarked, the nearest we can get to God is through a cloud of unknowing. And it was in silent meditation that St Augustine and his mother were able to communicate with God who is eternal, and words have a beginning and an end. Even Moses was unable ever to see God.

However, even though we can never know God we can believe and have Faith in Him. The reward of Faith is understanding. Therefore, we must not try to understand in order to believe, but believe in order to understand. As Paul said: 'Faith is the evidence of things unseen.'

Reason tells me that God did not create us just in order that we should live through our three score years and ten, and then return to dust from where we came. My faith tells me that I have a soul as well as a body. The body being of the earth is mortal and when we die returns to where it came from. But the soul is immortal and returns to where it came from. From God as I believe.

At 84 I have lived long enough and the prospect of death no longer appals me. Although I have done much that I should not have done and left undone many things which I should have done, I pray for forgiveness, and await my end hoping it will bring me to a closer walk with God.

Peter Ustinov CBE
Actor and writer

My concept of God is simply the best part of myself. But God and the Devil are part of a vast complicity. White and black as colours do not exist except as contrasts to each other. God and the Devil need each other as the lungs need air. They cannot survive alone. Their battleground is humanity, and there is no end to the conflict, or to the collusion. All either can ever hope for in this necessarily imperfect world is a democratic majority. In the words of an old Russian proverb 'Praise God, but do not neglect the Devil'.

I have no idea what happens when you die, but I hope to be able to tell you sooner or later, preferably later. When I was small, I used to believe that you were led into a huge hangar, there to be confronted by all that you had ever eaten in your life, miracu-lously reconstituted – mooing cows, grunting pigs, coming out of a jungle of vegetables. I have since begun to have my doubts about the likelihood of this possibility, although a certain squeamishness about the atrocious cruelty of nature persists.

I now tend to entertain thoughts of some form of reincarnation, or at least the continued existence of the soul beyond mortality, but perhaps this is merely because I am growing older, and more reluctant to consider life a mere question without an eventual answer. I can shape no convictions about life everlasting, however. I am sceptical in the face of conventional religious thinking, and can accept no belief as superior to any other. Nor can I agree that Socrates was unfortunate to live before Jesus Christ, and that the road to heaven is therefore barred to him. I have no preconceptions about either heaven or hell. However, I am prepared to be surprised at any moment. I am even prepared to consider the Last Judgement as most unfair, and if the after life should turn out to be exactly that depicted in religious paintings, I will be somewhat disappointed, to the extent of lodging an appeal.

Dr Ian Paisley MP, MEP

Leader of the Ulster Democratic Unionist Party

The only reliable authority upon which we can base our faith about God and the Hereafter is the Bible. The heavenliness of its matter, the efficacy of its doctrines, the majesty of its style and the discovery it makes of the only way of man's salvation, its many other incomparable excellencies and its entire perfection are evidences enough that it is what it claims to be – the Word of God.

To the willing heart, however, comes the Holy Spirit of God who bears witness in our hearts to the divinity of its origin and revelation. 'If any man will to do His will he shall *know*' (John 7:17).

God is a Spirit, infinite and unchangeable in His being, wisdom, power, holiness, justice, goodness and truth.

There is none beside Him, none before Him, none like Him, and none good save He.

God loves men and sent His Son to be the Saviour of the world.

The Bible tells us that after death there is judgement. The result of that judgement will be separation – the separation of those who received Christ as Saviour from those who rejected Him.

The saved ones shall be with Christ in a heaven of triumph forever. The lost ones shall be without Christ in a hell of torment forever.

Relationship not to the Church but to Christ, in time, settles our eternal destiny.

Seyed Mahdi al-Hakim (assassinated 1988)
Former Secretary General, World Ahl Ul-Bayt (A.S.) Islamic League

He is One in person. He is the only Creator. It is He alone who manages the world. It is He alone who deserves worship and adoration. He is One in many other aspects.

There is only One Supreme Lord of the universe. He is Omnipotent, Omniscient, Omnipresent and the Sustainer of the world. The Holy Qur'an says:

> Say: You may be sure that Allah is One. He is Needless (Independent). He begot none nor was He begotten. There is none like Him.
>
> (3:1-4)

from *Philosophy of Islam* by Ayatullah Dr Muhammad Hosayni Behishti and Hujjatul-Islam Dr Javad Bahonar, Islamic Publications.

As a Muslim I believe there is life after death. All human beings, irrespective of their view of life, their belief or creed, are unanimous in their judgement that each and every one of them will one day part with this world. Yet they try in their own different ways to formulate a kind of immortality for themselves in this life. This, of course, is an outwardly erroneous expression of an inner feeling of the human being's tendency to be immortal. Islam goes along with such a tendency but it caters for the right controls so that men do not go astray. Saying 'When a man dies he is cut from this life save for 3 things; a continuous charity work or a knowledge which could benefit his fellow human beings, or a good offspring praying to Allah for his forgiveness.' Thus Islam wants to fulfil this need for immortality which besets the human mind by saying you will die, but this does not mean that you may sever your links with this world. Man's stay in this world is a transition from one state of being to another and he needs continuous rationing for the hereafter which is the real life.

From here stems our concept of resurrection. The following Qur'anic verse sums up the idea:

> O people! If you are in doubt about the raising, then surely We created you from dust, then from a small seed, then from a clot, then from a lump of flesh. Complete in make and incomplete, what We may make clear to you; and We cause what We please to stay in the wombs till an appointed time, then We bring you forth as babies, then that you may attain your maturity; and of you is he who is caused to die, and of you is he who is brought back to the worst part of life, so that after having knowledge he does not know anything; and you see the earth sterile land, but when We send down on it water, it stirs and swells and brings forth of every kind a beautiful herbage.
>
> This is because Allah is the Truth and because He gives life to the dead and because He has power over all things.
>
> And because the hour is coming, there is no doubt about it; and because Allah shall raise up those who are in the graves.
>
> (22:5–7)

See how the verse tells about the different phases of life.

There are other areas where the concept of resurrection forms an integral part. The first is that which relates to religion. It is the leverage which makes man adhere to the commandments of God for if he were not to believe in the day of judgement after death, he would have never had the incentive to practise religious teachings or refrain from what God has decreed illicit.

The second is that of resurrection and divine justice. We know that God is just. Thus this concept does not stick unless it is correlated with the concept of divine justice in that some of us in this life are either oppressed or oppressors and that justice has not been done in our lifetime. Who is going to do us justice and when? If we rule out the concept of divine justice this means that the oppressed would not get his right back and that the oppressor would not be retributed because this is symmetrically opposed to the idea that God is just.

The third notion is that of resurrection and legislative power. Since our being forms an integral part of other beings in the universe and we influence and are influenced by other systems, there must be a need for a super knowledgeable being (God) to legislate for us so as to hold the balance between these interdependent systems. Man cannot be the source of such power because of his limited ability and vision, for regardless of what humanity has achieved in terms of civilization and knowledge it remains lacking in comprehending its needs. Thus it needs the guidance of Allah because He alone knows best the relationship between man and other entities surrounding him. So He should be the source of legislation. The following Qur'anic verses sum up this meaning:

> Say: O Allah! Originator of the heavens and the earth, Knower of the unseen and seen! Thou (only) judgest between Thy servants as to that wherein they differ.
>
> (39:46)

This denotes that there is an umbilical cord between the life in this world and the hereafter.

The fourth is that of resurrection and egoism. Egoism is one of those innate needs because man is bound to covet things for himself. This world is too small to meet our needs and expectations. Consequently conflict, oppression and injustice ensue and if we believe in resurrection a fundamental thing is resolved because the concept is in line with the human innate disposition. Furthermore if egoism is not harnessed it would be manipulated towards evil ends. But if under the concept of resurrection it turns out to be a good tool.

Jeremy Isaacs

Director General, The Royal Opera House

On the whole, I prefer to keep my ideas on God to myself, but for the sake of the good cause that you are working for, I will reply to the two questions that you put. My answers are:

None

Nothing

PEANUTS   by Schulz

The Archbishop of Canterbury
The Most Rev. and Rt Hon. Dr Robert Runcie

◆§ · §◆

I know what God is like because I know from the gospels what Jesus was like. I often think of the words of one of my predecessors: 'God is Christ-like and in him is no unChristlikeness at all.'

We are secure because in death we shall be still in the care of the One we've learnt to trust and who doesn't let us down.

Lord Charles Forte
Chairman, Trust House Forte

◆§ · §◆

I believe absolutely in the Kingdom of Heaven, but for me paradise is God's great gift of life and all the wondrous things around us. I have not made an advance reservation into the beyond and indeed, when the time to depart on that journey does come, I shall do so with some reluctance. I am certain that Heaven (and I am confident I will not be sent elsewhere) will be a beautiful place, but I have no fixed conception of what it will be like. I am prepared to be pleasantly surprised.

◆§ · §◆

Everybody wants to go to heaven, but nobody wants to die.
Joe Louis

Jeffrey Archer

Politician and author

If there is a God, and with so much unhappiness and unfairness in the world one is bound to wonder if there is one, I would see him as all caring, understanding and I hope with a sense of humour.

I have no idea what happens to one when you die, I can only hope that God will allow me to sit on top of the Lords Pavilion so that I may watch the odd Test match in my spare time. Though I suppose he might compel me to years of watching Sumo wrestling.

Ken Livingstone MP

I am an atheist, and believe in the evolution of time, and when we die 'We are dead', to quote Bertrand Russell.

I could prove God statistically.
George Gallup

Patrick Moore OBE
Astronomer

⇌ · ⇋

My concept of God is NOT a supreme being who will tolerate the World Council of Churches (backed by the Church of England) in its continuing support and organization of murder and terrorism in Southern Africa.

We go on to Stage 2! If Life ended here, it would be pointless.

Patric Walker
Astrologer

All I know for sure about God is that it isn't me.

I believe that we're not punished for our sins but by them.

Dr Jonathan Miller CBE
Film director and theatrical producer

I have no more concept of God than I have of snarks or slithy toves. In fact, I find it a great deal easier to imagine these than I do in conceiving, visualizing or imagining God, whoever he, she, or whatever might be. In fact, I'm not even sure I can make sense of the concept of being for such a Being, or if you want it the other way round, what being for such a Being might be.

The whole point about dying, as far as I can see, is that it's the *end* of things happening to you. After dying you are no longer around for things to happen. I've never been able to make sense of the suggestion that one survives one's bodily death, although I've always been intrigued by the suggestion that if one's been bad during life – not very bad, but quite bad – then one comes back immediately after death, trapped in some alternative form of social existence which one would previously have found quite unacceptable. In several early stories illustrating the emerging concept of purgatory, this alternative posthumous identity took the form of bath attendant in some obscure tepidarium in fourth-century Ravenna, but since I don't believe anything of this, I have, I suppose, nothing to fear.

Bailey R. Irani
Zoroastrian Association of Europe

Zarathustra (or Zoroaster to use the graecized version) is considered by many to be the first monotheist. He was born in ancient Persia; no-one can be certain exactly when, but it was probably around the same time that the early Jewish people, some Hindus and Akhenaten in Egypt were conceiving of their one God. Zarathustra's wholly good creator God was Ahura Mazda, the God of Light.

Zarathustra though is also known for his dualism. Darkness or the evil spirit exists within the universe, and life is a battlefield: a struggle between good and evil. I, as a Zoroastrian, aim to be a co-fighter with good, but I can freely choose to side with evil. Zarathustra taught however that finally good will overcome evil, and Ahura Mazda reigns supreme.

Zarathustra was also a great believer in the justice of Ahura Mazda and in life after death. At death, the soul comes to a judgement bridge where its good and evil thoughts, words and deeds are weighed. If the good weighs more, the soul crosses the bridge to paradise. If not, it has to endure purgatory. This might suggest that one should merely tot up good and expect paradise. However, a good thing, according to Zarathustra, is one done without thought of reward but for its own sake. The highest good is the Truth; the greatest evil, the Lie. Zarathustra, as well as being known for his monotheism and dualism, is also the first great moralist, and the first to emphasize the primacy of Truth.

I am proud to be a Zoroastrian. Zarathustra is my prophet, and his God, Ahura Mazda, is my God. I wear the sacred vest and cord – the 'Sudrah' and 'Kusti' – and always pray to Ahura Mazda in the ancient 'Avestan' language when I rise in the morning, and before I sleep. I also worship him in the Zoroastrian places of worship: the Fire Temples. Fire is one of Ahura Mazda's holiest creations, the symbol of purity, in which all evil things are burnt away. A fire reminds a Zoroastrian of the power of purity.

We Zoroastrians are few, but we have survived for thousands of years with the message of Zarathustra still burning in our hearts. And we shall live on. Our faith and fire shall never die.

B.C.   by johnny hart

Commander M. B. S. *Higham*

Grand Secretary, United Grand Lodge of England

◦§ · §◦

I am a very ordinary, middle of the road, Church of England type but I am also Grand Secretary of the United Grand Lodge of England.

I am not, as a Freemason, allowed to express any opinion on theological matters and it would be very difficult for me to contribute to your admirable enterprise as a person without breaking our rules, so I hope you will understand if I do not answer your questions.

◦§ · §◦

From *Appendix B* of letter from President to members of the United Grand Lodge of England, 1985:

BASIC STATEMENT

Freemasonry is not a religion, nor is it a substitute for religion. It demands of its members belief in a Supreme Being, but provides no system of faith of its own. Its rituals include prayers, but these relate only to the matter instantly in hand and do not amount to the practice of a religion.

Freemasonry is open to men of any faith, but religion may not be discussed at its meetings.

THE SUPREME BEING

The names used for the Supreme Being enable men of different faiths to join in prayer (to God as they see Him) without the terms of the prayer causing dissension among them.

There is no Masonic God; a Freemason remains committed to the God of the religion he professes.

Freemasons meet in common respect for the Supreme Being, but He remains Supreme in their individual religions, and it is no part of Freemasonry to attempt to join religions together. There is therefore no composite Masonic God.

Sir Richard Body MP
◄§ · §►

I agree with Spinoza. First anathemized, then expelled from the synagogue and though he lived in Holland, the one country in the 17th century where there was a degree of religious freedom, his more important books could not be published until after his death; and when they were he was denounced as a most heinous atheist by all and sundry.

Spinoza got himself into trouble for saying God was infinite and, logically, He must be everywhere in the universe; that to deny His presence anywhere was to question His infinite nature. It follows God must be the cause of everything that happens, even the things we consider to be bad and evil.

Spinoza denied that this was pantheism: God does not take the form of any physical matter. He is, however, the sum total of all the laws that govern the universe. Philosophers used to draw the distinction between *natura naturans* and *natura naturata*. The latter is all that we can see and touch – nature as she is formed. The invisible force, the spirit power creating that form is *natura naturans* – and it is God.

A humanist or an atheist would not demur from that, for he would simply say it made God an unnecessary, extra word. But Spinoza was not thinking of just the laws of physical science. True, the law of gravity is God's law; and like all His laws not to be broken; but important though they are, it is the laws of human behaviour that matter above all else. It is here where Spinoza parts company with the atheist and becomes a Christian.

The laws of how we should behave are in the pages of the Gospels and distilled in the Sermon on the Mount. Now when we are in breach of a law laid down by Act of Parliament or some statutory regulation which has no moral ground, our lives may carry on as before, provided we are not caught. The laws laid down in the Gospels are not of this kind: our lives change when we are in breach of them: they have a moral ground, and the consequences of disobeying them are as certain and inexorable as an attempt to defy the law of gravity.

Why does some burglar persistently break into other people's houses? What has made him into that kind of character? His conduct is caused, as everything in the universe is caused; and each cause is part of a long chain going back infinitely. No one cause has made the burglar the man he is; a mix of many causes have blended together.

Although Jesus could get angry – as on the occasion He overthrew the tables of the traders in the temple – He nonetheless warned us of how pointless it was to become angry with others. We may not like what they have done; indeed it may be right to hate the deed; but it is never, in any circumstances, right to hate another. We must separate the actor from the action; and intensely difficult though it may be, success in doing so goes to the heart of the Christian message.

Both of the essential Commandments come into play when we make the attempt to separate the actor and the action. The infinite number of causes which have induced Black to break into White's house are the results of various laws of human behaviour. They are thus the work of God. This may seem a terrible heresy for it suggests that God is a wilful cause of evil. The proper interpretation is, I believe, the very opposite. Jesus enjoined us to 'fear God', not to be frightened of Him but to realize that if we disobeyed His laws about how we should behave, a succession of disagreeable consequences would follow; and do so with certainty.

The all-important law of loving our neighbour is placed high upon a special pedestal because it is, indeed, all important. Any lapse, even a slight transgression, will bounce back upon us hurting us as well as others. A single lapse will lead on to a succession of causes and effects, like ripples in a pond from where the stone falls, gradually diminishing in effect.

The transgression of the law of love of which we are guilty is, of course, itself the effect of a cause. If a long chain of cause and effect has induced us to do this wrong to our neighbour, does it not deny freedom or will? Indeed, it does.

Many Christians will resile from such a conclusion. A determinist view of human nature suggests as everything that happens in our lives has been mapped out long ago, there is nothing we can do to alter the chain of events. So sit back and let the world go by.

Although at first sight it may seem easy to parody the

determinist point of view, we have to recognize that just as there is a chain of events which leads Black to be a burglar, there is another which took Mother Teresa to the slums of Calcutta.

As Quakers say 'there is that of God in all of us', whether they are what we may choose to call 'good' or 'bad'. Both, however, are relative terms to measure how people behave towards us. To understand that their behaviour has been determined by God's laws or by God Himself is to see the importance of separating a regard for someone else from his or her behaviour. The deeds done we can approve, deplore or treat with indifference. But for the human being who has done the deed there can be only one kind of regard; and that is love. Happiness (which is something very different from pleasure) comes to us when we abide by that. So far as my experience goes, that is always the case, that this law of love is just as certain and just as inevitable as the law of gravity. What more proof do I need or could I have that God exists?

Erich von Däniken
Author of *Chariots of the Gods*

⋅

GOD is creation, is the beginning and the end. GOD is wave, is atom, is molecule. GOD is life and death, GOD is everything and every creature on every planet in this universe. GOD is timeless and eternal. Nobody was ever able to describe GOD. The greatness of GOD is so unbelievable, that man can not understand it.

Science has established that nothing can vanish without a trace. There is no destruction in nature, only transformation. And the famous Nobel-prizewinner Max Planck (1858–1947), who opened up new paths to physics with his quantum theory, admitted:

As a physicist, i.e. as a man who has devoted his life to the most matter of fact branch of science – namely, the investigation of matter, I am surely free of any suspicion of fanaticism. And so after my research into the atom I say this to you: there is no such thing as matter per se! All matter originates from and consists of a force which sets the atomic particles in oscillation and concentrates them into the minute solar system of the atom. But as there is neither an intelligence nor an internal force in the whole universe, we must assume a conscious intelligent spirit behind this force. This spirit is the basic principle of all matter . . .

I believe that there is always a life after death. Every one of us has already had thousands and thousands of lives and will have thousands and thousands of lives in the future. This goes from eternity to eternity, because we are all part of the creation, which is infinite.

Lyall Watson

Biologist and author

As a biologist, I can be sure of very little about life; except that it is a rare and unreasonable thing, with some very disturbing habits.

Probability theory allows life, however improbable it may be in a disorderly universe, to begin. And the theory of evolution describes ways in which such seeds, once sown, could grow into millions of distinctive forms. But for any naturalist with a lively mind, these theories never go quite far enough. Life too often succeeds, against the odds and despite the strictures of natural selection, in getting things incredibly right in a very short space of time. There is a ghost in the machinery of living things that remains to be laid.

In many respects, our Earth is unexceptional. It may well be typical of a number of similar planets in place around comparable stars. But the fact is that it is solid and situated near a steady Sun, when most of the universe is in a gaseous and highly unstable state, totally incapable of allowing the luxuries of atmosphere and ocean. We and our world are the result, it seems, of a long chain of wildly improbable cosmic coincidences which lie within, but yet cannot be contained by, the laws of nature. There are gaps in our understanding of all this that yearn for gods to fill them. And there are, of course, more than enough gods to go round.

Mine is a bit odd and rather personal. Not so much omniscient as omnifarious. A god of many parts who conspires to arrange affairs, in this corner of the cosmos at least, for the benefit of living things. Who picks order out of the prevailing chaos, exercising an extraordinary bias in favour of constructive accidents, starting processes, forming patterns, making sense, creating a world which owes as much to music as it does to mathematics. And I love the result.

It may not all make sense, but even the mysteries – *especially* the mysteries – seem sensible. They fit. I feel a deep sense of satisfaction with the way things are, the way they are designed to be. I might miss the meaning, but the measure is fine. The patterns please, I think, because we are all natural products of the system. And if any of us turn out to be intelligent beings, then it can only be because we are fruits of an intelligent earth, which is nourished in its turn by an intelligent system of energy.

I am touched by the magic here and see no need for special places or occasions for prayer. There are choirs enough to the dawn chorus and cathedrals full of fellow celebrants in every drop of dew. There is no room in my theology for doctrine or ordination. All one needs is a sense of awe, an ability to look at things with wide eyes and see that we did not come into this world, but *out* of it, like butterflies out of cocoons. And we fulfil our life cycles which end, not in heaven or in hell, but back in the system, ready once again to cock an unlikely snook at the laws of thermodynamics.

My god, therefore, is good only in the sense that ecologies in equilibrium are the ones that bloom; and wrathful in that those which are abused, soon die. And my religion is one without profound revelations, except perhaps the one which holds that worship, when you stop to think about it, is nothing more or less than a deep and proper sense of self-respect.

Carl Sagan
Scientist and author

◆§ · ἒ◆

There are many legitimate scientific issues relating to origins and ends: What is the origin of the human species? Where did plants and animals come from? how did life arise? the Earth, the planets, the Sun, the stars? Does the universe have an origin, and if so, why? And finally, a still more fundamental and exotic question, which many scientists would say is essentially untestable and therefore meaningless: Why are the laws of nature the way they are? The idea that a God or gods is necessary to effect one or more of these origins has been under repeated attack over the last few thousand years. Because we know something about phototropism and plant hormones, we can understand the opening of the morning glory independent of divine microintervention. It is the same for the entire skein of causality back to the origin of the universe. As we learn more and more about the universe, there seems less and less for God to do.

. . . Let us consider the idea of a universe created somehow from nothing by God. The question naturally arises – and many ten-year-olds spontaneously think of it before being discouraged by their elders – where does God come from? If we answer that God is infinitely old or present simultaneously in all epochs, we have solved nothing, except perhaps verbally. We have merely postponed by one step coming to grips with the problem. A universe that is infinitely old and a God that is infinitely old are, I think, equally deep mysteries. It is not readily apparent why one should be considered more reliably established than the others. Spinoza might have said that the two possibilities are not really different ideas at all.

I think it is wise, when coming face to face with such profound mysteries, to feel a little humility. The idea that scientists or theologians, with our present still puny understanding of this vast and awesome cosmos, can comprehend the origins of the universe is only a little less silly than the idea that Mesopotamian astronomers of 3,000 years ago – from whom the ancient Hebrews borrowed, during the Babylonian captivity, the cosmological accounts in the first chapter of Genesis – could have understood the origins of the universe. We simply do not know.

If we look at the universe in the large, we find something astonishing. First of all, we find a universe that is exceptionally beautiful, intricately and subtly constructed. Whether our appreciation of the universe is because we are part of that universe – whether, no matter how the universe were put together, we would have found it beautiful – is a proposition to which I do not pretend to have an answer. But there is no question that the elegance of the universe is one of its most remarkable properties. At the same time, there is no question that there are cataclysms and catastrophes occurring regularly in the universe and on the most awesome scale. There are, for example, quasar explosions which probably decimate the nuclei of galaxies. It seems likely that every time a quasar explodes, more than a million worlds are obliterated and countless forms of life, some of them intelligent, are utterly destroyed. This is not the traditional benign universe of conventional religiosity in the West, constructed for the benefit of living and especially of human beings. Indeed, the very scale of the universe – more than a hundred billion galaxies, each containing more than a hundred billion stars – speaks to us of the inconsequentiality of human events in the cosmic context. We see a universe simultaneously very beautiful and very violent. We see a universe that does not exclude a traditional Western or Eastern god, but that does not require one either.

My deeply held belief is that if a god of anything like the traditional sort exists, our curiosity and intelligence are provided by such a god. We would be unappreciative of those gifts (as well as unable to take such a course of action) if we suppressed our passion to explore the universe and ourselves. On the other hand, if such a traditional god does not exist, our curiosity and our intelligence are the essential tools for managing our survival. In either case, the enterprise of knowledge is consistent with both science and religion, and is essential for the welfare of the human species.

Those who raise questions about the God hypothesis and the soul hypothesis are by no means all atheists. An atheist is someone who is certain that God does not exist, someone who has compelling evidence against the existence of God. I know of no such compelling evidence. Because God can be relegated to remote times and places and to ultimate causes, we would have to know a great deal more about the universe than we do now to be sure that no such God exists. To be certain of the existence of God and to be certain of the nonexistence of God seem to me to be the confident extremes in a subject so riddled with doubt and uncertainty as to inspire very little confidence indeed. A wide range of intermediate positions seems admissible, and considering the enormous emotional energies with which the subject is invested, a questing, courageous and open mind seems to be the essential tool for narrowing the range of our collective ignorance on the subject of the existence of God.

William Wolcott died and went to heaven. Or so it seemed. Before being wheeled to the operating table, he had been reminded that the surgical procedure would entail a certain risk. The operation was a success, but just as the anaesthesia was wearing off his heart went into fibrillation and he died. It seemed to him that he had somehow left his body and was able to look down upon it, withered and pathetic, covered only by a sheet, lying on a hard and unforgiving surface. He was only a little sad, regarded his body one last time – from a great height, it seemed – and continued a kind of upward journey. While his surroundings had been suffused by a strange permeating darkness, he realized that things were now getting brighter – looking up, you might say. And then he was being illuminated from a distance, flooded with light. He entered a kind of radiant kingdom and there, just ahead of him, he could make out in silhouette, magnificently lit from behind, a great godlike figure whom he was now effortlessly approaching. Wolcott strained to make out His face . . .

And then awoke. In the hospital operating room where the defibrillation machine had been rushed to him, he had been resuscitated at the last possible moment. Actually, his heart had stopped, and by some definitions of this poorly understood process, he had died. Wolcott was certain that he *had* died, that he had been vouchsafed a glimpse of life after death and a confirmation of Judaeo-Christian theology.

Similar experiences, now widely documented by physicians and others, have occurred all over the world. These perithanatic, or near-death, epiphanies have been experienced not only by people of conventional Western religiosity but also by Hindus and Buddhists and sceptics. It seems plausible that many of our conventional ideas about heaven are derived from such near-death experiences, which must have been related regularly over the millennia. No news could have been more interesting or more hopeful than that of the traveller returned, the report that there is a voyage and a life after death, that there is a God who awaits us, and that upon death we feel grateful and uplifted, awed and overwhelmed.

For all I know, these experiences may be just what they seem and a vindication of the pious faith that has taken such a pummelling from science in the past few centuries. Personally, I would be delighted if there were a life after death – especially if it permitted me to continue to learn about this world and others, if it gave me a chance to discover how history turns out. But I am also a scientist, so I think about what other explanations are possible. How could it be that people of all ages, cultures and eschatological predispositions have the *same sort* of near-death experience?

We know that similar experiences can be induced with fair regularity, cross-culturally, by psychedelic drugs. Out-of-body experiences are induced by dissociative anaesthetics such as the ketamines (2-[o-chlorophenyl]-2-[methylamino] cyclohexanones). The illusion of flying is induced by atropine and other belladonna alkaloids, and these molecules, obtained, for example, from mandrake or jimson weed, have been used regularly by European witches and North American *curanderos* ('healers') to experience, in the midst of religious ecstasy, soaring and glorious flight. MDA (2,4-methylenedioxyamphetamine) tends to induce age regression, an accessing of experiences from youth and infancy which we had thought entirely forgotten. DMT (N,N-dimethyltryptamine) induces micropsia and macropsia, the sense of the world shrinking or expanding, respectively – a little like what happens to Alice after she obeys instructions on small containers reading 'Eat me' or 'Drink me'. LSD (lysergic acid diethylamide) induces a sense of union with the universe, as in the identification of Brahman with Atman in Hindu religious belief.

Can it really be that the Hindu mystical experience is prewired into us, requiring only 200 micrograms of LSD to be made manifest? If something like ketamine is released in times of mortal danger or near-death, and people returning from such an experience always provide the same account of heaven and God, then must there not be a sense in which Western as well as Eastern religions are hard-wired in the neuronal architecture of our brains?

It is difficult to see why evolution should have selected brains that are predisposed to such experiences, since no one seems to die or fail to reproduce from a want of mystic fervour. Might these drug-inducible experiences as well as the near-death epiphany be due merely to some evolutionarily neutral wiring defect in the brain which, by accident, occasionally brings forth altered perceptions of the world? That possibility, it seems to me, is extremely implausible, and perhaps no more than a desperate rationalist attempt to avoid a serious encounter with the mystical.

The only alternative, so far as I can see, is that every human being, without exception, has already shared an experience like that of those travellers who return from the land of death: the sensation of flight; the emergence from darkness into light; an experience in which, at least sometimes, a heroic figure can be dimly perceived, bathed in radiance and glory. There is only one common experience that matches this description. It is called birth.

from *Broca's Brain: Reflections on the Romance of Science*, Random House, 1978.

Dr *Albert Hofmann*
Research chemist, discoverer of LSD

᪷ ᪷ ᪷

I believe in a creator and sustainer of the cosmos and of all life, in a creative spirit which we name God.

I believe that He is unveiling His message to His creatures

who are able to receive it, to human beings, by His creation which is a message of eternal life behind alteration of birth and death, a message of joy and love expressed by the endlessness of the starry sky and by the beauty of innumerable living organisms of the plant and animal kingdom on our wonderful blue planet Earth.

I believe that by my consciousness, the divine gift granted to every human being, I am connected with God, secured in His spiritual kingdom.

I believe, that when I die, I return to the source of all life, to God.

Colin Field

President, National Association of Funeral Directors

As an active member of the Church of England with what I regard as an active faith (I don't know if the Vicar shares that view), it would be all too easy to start pushing my opinions forward sermon style. In my profession though I have to be mindful of the feelings and thoughts of others.

It would be too easy to share some of the expressions that have been shared with me by those whom I hope I have helped, but would it be right to tell you of the horrors of hell which those who have sinned are permanently consigned to, complete with furnace stoking! Or, would you prefer to know that heaven is full of trumpeters, presumably they don't sleep up there, if that is where it is.

In my usual manner, can I answer the last question first and that way buy time to consider my answer to the first; I do believe in heaven and I do believe that we all go there and yes, I do believe it exists out beyond the sky, yet I have no idea why astronauts have not yet found it.

My belief is in truth that in heaven we are all reunited with our families and with those whom we have loved, to live in peace without pain or suffering. We take up from where we left each other and resume our relationships as if without a break. We are all ageless and by that I believe that at whatever point our earthly clock stops that is the age we take with us forever into a perfectly balanced community, one where the underlying sound is of children's happiness and contentment, just like in the preparatory school playground, away from fear or worry, enjoying total security.

Since I was first asked a similar question, I must admit to a certain apprehension over the limitations of heaven and the ability of God to continue to take us all in, but that I suppose is because heaven has and knows no limits, doesn't have planners, politicians or supermarkets. Still, it is a surprise that the astronauts haven't found it yet, and still I hope they won't – well not in my lifetime anyway.

To return to the first question, I have honestly to admit that I have no idea what to expect or even whom to look for, especially if I was called tomorrow. I would, therefore, content myself by searching out my family, especially my Mother for I do feel that not only will she be waiting to greet me, she will know I'm on my way. No, she I know is not God nor do I think is anyone else; she will, however, know her way around, will set me on the right course of do's and don'ts, and will tell me she has not met her Maker either.

There is good and love in each of us and happiness, laughter, sickness and sorrow; all of these feelings are part of God, we are part of him and his work, he made us and when he is ready he will take us away. So I suppose I should say, believe that you and I are part of him and he is part of us here as in heaven, and it does not matter whose heaven or by what name we know him, we all are talking to, with and about the same person.

ৡ · ৡ

Death is a stage in human progress, to be passed as we would pass from childhood to youth, or from youth to manhood, and with the same consciousness of an everlasting nature.

E. H. Sears

Vincent Price
Actor

❦ · ❧

God is the plan! All life, thought and even fantasy works according to that plan.

Death is as much a part of the plan as life – it is the purification of life.

Bill Jordan
President, Amalgamated Engineering Union

❦ · ❧

I have decided to resist Alexander Pope's advice 'Know then thyself, presume not God to scan' and would say my concept of God is shaped by the infinite variety of life and the inorganic structures that earth holds, together with the unimaginable number of Suns, Planets and miles in the known Universe. If God made all this, he must be an Engineer (Universal, of course).

I only pray that when I die there will be no pickets at the Pearly Gates, only a sign saying 'Vacancies – Apply Within (Conditions include Single Status)'.

❦ · ❧

Michael Palin

Actor, comedian

There once was a fellow called God
Who everyone thought rather odd,
Apart from a lady
Called Eileen O'Grady
Who worshipped the ground that he trod

from *Limericks*, Hutchinson, 1985

Who or what is God?

Someone you know is always there even if you don't believe in him.

What happens when we die?

No more phone calls.

The Bishop of London
The Rt Rev. Graham Leonard

The Christian Gospel, which I believe and by which I try to live, is about God. It tells that he has revealed himself to us and shows us what he is like at the very heart of his being.

God is not an impersonal force or a solitary being albeit of supreme goodness. He is love – not just loving but love itself from whom all human love is derived. He calls men and women whom he creates to share in that love.

No one can be compelled to love. Love by its nature demands the freedom to respond or to reject. God loves us even when we reject him. The cost of doing so is seen on the Cross when in Christ he accepts the results of our rejection while loving us to the full.

The Christian who is called to share that love is also called to accept the cost of doing so in a wounded and distorted world. But he knows that love is ultimately victorious as he lives in and with the risen Christ and that by the creative forgiveness of God men and women can be healed and fulfilled.

So, committing myself into God's hands, I believe that when I die I shall be taken into the love of God in a new and deeper way. I shall be cleansed and renewed. What is not of God in me will be purged away and what is of God in me will be brought to fulfilment in company with all redeemed in Christ. So I hope then to be exercised in the whole of my being to the glory of God sharing his love in a life which is one both of perfect activity and perfect rest.

Geoffrey Bourne

Professor of Nutrition and Vice Chancellor, St George's University, Grenada, West Indies

In the time of the ancient Greeks Plato regarded the stars and the planets as spiritual entities, that they were created by a divine being and that they influenced affairs on earth. A writer in the 9th century, John Scot extended this view by saying that the whole of Nature was nothing but a manifestation of God and this conception is held by many millions of people all over the world at the present day.

The question which comes up is 'Is God reality, or is he the product of a thinking brain?' The same question might be asked of the soul. We are unable, even now, with all our technology to decide what is the soul or where it is located. The only thing we know of which might even 'remotely' be thought of as a soul, and I emphasize 'remotely', is the DNA (deoxyribonucleic acid) which every cell in the body contains. It is our individual DNA which decides who and what we are. If our genes have the DNA which produces humans, the mother who bears us will produce a human, not a goat or a chimpanzee or a rabbit. In fact, as has been done, if the fertilized egg from another woman is implanted in a woman's uterus, the child will have the characteristics of the mother who provided the egg not of the mother who bears the child.

The mother who bears a child will produce one unlike any other human unless there is an identical twin formed by the splitting of the eggs and the passing on to the twin of an identical set of DNA.

The DNA produces the body and brain according to a pattern

for which it has the directives. On these basic patterns, the environment sets to work and modifies them in various ways. Our 'soul', if it is the DNA, can be passed on to our children and the souls of two parents blend in the child. In this way our soul (our DNA) can be passed on from generation to generation. Is this really what is meant by immortality?

Maybe we achieve immortality in another way. When we look at the sun we are not seeing it as it was at that moment but as it looked seven seconds ago – we are seeing now what was a bit of the sun's history. When we look at the planet Jupiter we are seeing it as it was 20 minutes or so ago. If we had a station on Jupiter with a powerful enough telescope we would see a bit of the world's history from 20 minutes to half an hour after it happened. If we moved further and further out into space with more and more powerful telescopes we could see what had happened on the earth a year, ten years, a thousand years ago as if it was happening now. From the right position in space with the right telescope we could see the first atomic bomb being dropped as if it were being dropped at that instant. If the telescopes or other sensors which might be developed were powerful enough they could pick out individual people to see them carrying out their lives many years after they have died as if they were alive at the time they were being observed. Everything we are seeing in the sky is history; we are not seeing anything that 'is' at the moment of viewing. We can be looking at some star for the next 100 or 1000 years before it will disappear from the sky although it was long gone – so time and existence and reality are all relative. The visual 'history' of individuals and of our earth is passing further out into space – from far enough out you could see the origin of the earth and from outside our Universe the origin of the Universe. Is immortality simply our image passing further and further out into space?

Immortality is presumably conferred upon us by God and in the sense that he is responsible for the natural physical laws this could be so for the type of immortality which we suggest. This brings us to the nature of God and his role.

Raymond Drake in his book *Gods and Spacemen in Ancient East* says 'Science with all its wonderful instruments perceives only a narrow slit in the real universe, only God can know his whole creation'. So we are faced with the question 'What is God and what is his role in creation?' The famous astronomer, Sir James Jeans, referring to the origin of the Universe indicated that it may have been formed when 'the finger of God stirred the ether'. Most of the religions, Egyptian, Chinese, Christian, ancient Indian, etc. picture their Gods as human-like beings, many of whom descended to the earth in fiery chariots. The conception of God as being of the same appearance and nature as man is widespread. God is invariably figured as a man in illustrations depicting God, probably largely due to the fact that the concept of God grew up in male-dominated societies. The Bible says that God created man in his own image. Jesus was the son of God and it is of interest but not surprising, that God did not send his only beloved daughter as a prophet.

The concept of God today is therefore one of a father figure full of compassion and love, someone from whom individuals could seek help in making decisions, to whom they could consign their cares, someone whom they could enlist in solving their earthly problems, someone who is so all powerful and all knowing that the death of a sparrow does not go unnoticed by him.

I personally find it very hard to conceive of God as a human-like figure with the same behaviour and mental processes as man. The existence of heaven and hell and a devil seems to belong to the mediaeval concept of God and religion. Before we knew so much about space it was natural to conceive of heaven as being 'up there' somewhere in the 'sky' and that hell was somewhere 'down there' in the bowels of the earth, where volcanoes have indicated to us that horrible and searing heat prevails.

God created the world and all the bodies in the heavens we are told, and they obey his laws in their movements. We know that 'something' is responsible for the physical laws which the earth and other planetary bodies and the molecules and atoms obey. Even behaviour which does not at first look orderly, such as the appearance and disappearance of comets is in fact governed by physical laws. The astronomer Halley who discovered the comet named after him in 1682 was able to predict on the basis of Newton's laws of gravity that it would reappear in 1758, which it did.

The Universe is said to be expanding – expanding into what? Expanding into nothingness? Are there other universes? Our brains cannot really grasp this or the significance of it, we cannot conceive of eternity or never-ending space – we cannot in fact really understand the concept of God; that is why we reduce God to a concept we can understand – a father figure. God must be the force which caused the formation of the Universe and which laid down the laws which all matter in the Universe follows. Is this 'super force' what we really mean by 'God'? Our brains have not yet evolved to a level which would enable us to comprehend the true nature and significance of that 'force'. We await the evolution of a brain or brains that will permit us to comprehend it all – just as we had to await a Newton in 1687 to explain to us about gravity and its laws, and an Einstein to make us aware of the relationship between energy and mass.

From Einstein we know that an energy force can produce mass and that is how the solid matter of the Universe was produced; it can just as easily, under the right conditions, go back to energy. Whether the force which produced our Universe is a force for 'good' – in other words 'God', we cannot know for certain. Was it 'good' that the Universe was produced? Is the production of matter from energy 'good'? Is matter 'good' and anti-matter 'evil'? Conceptually we could say that matter and anti-matter are the equivalents of God and Satan, but factually this does not get us anywhere.

In conclusion I must say that I do not feel that I need a personal God to whom I must account for my day to day actions. What I try to do as I operate my life is to follow a code of conduct which I feel at least a Christian God would approve; I try not to hurt or harm mentally or physically another human being, I respect and love God's animals and try to be understanding and kind to them but never to casually hurt them – I am against hurting in any form. I do not know whether God is even especially interested in human beings or their fate. I believe God may be a force that is concerned with things on a much greater scale – the beginning and end of universes, the creator of cosmic events and that life is a by-product of his divine manipulation.

Belief of God is acceptance of the basic principle that the universe makes sense, that there is behind it an ultimate purpose.

Carl Wallace Miller

Stephen Hawking CBE
Professor of Applied Mathematics and Physics,
University of Cambridge

I don't believe in a personal god.

When I die, I'm dead.

The Venerable Sangharakshita
The Western Buddhist Order

As a Buddhist I have no concept of God, though I do believe in the existence of a higher spiritual reality which cannot be adequately described either in personal or impersonal terms.

When we die we are reborn in accordance with our actions, either here on earth or elsewhere – unless we have attained to a higher state of existence where such terms as birth and death no longer have any meaning.

Jean Davies
Chairman, The Voluntary Euthanasia Society

To me the world makes a lot more sense without assuming that there is someone called 'God'. I was brought up to be a Christian but I found it more and more difficult to agree with a religious interpretation of natural phenomena and human history as I began to read more widely. Finally, when I was about seventeen I thought 'There isn't any god', cringed momentarily as I waited for the thunderbolt, and have never looked back.

As mankind developed it was natural that early man should have been awestruck by the power of the sun and wind, puzzled by sudden illness and the arbitrariness of accidents, and should have attributed it all to the activity of a supernatural being. Men then had a chance of controlling events by pleading with, pleasing or bribing this powerful figure. Few people now, it seems to me, interpret the world and how they should behave in it, in religious terms. They certainly don't talk or behave as if they do.

When we die that is the end of us, in my view. It will be exactly like being asleep or unconscious, but without ever waking up. As far as I am concerned after my death will be the same experience as before my conception, i.e. nothingness.

The world and the people in it fill me with wonder, delight and satisfaction, as well as occasional grief and exasperation. They are enough for me; I don't need anyone to worship or pray to, and I certainly wouldn't want to live for ever.

Mother Teresa of Calcutta

God is my Father who loves me.

I will go home to God and I will be judged on my love for Him in the poor – I was hungry you gave me to eat, I was thirsty, you gave me to drink, I was homeless you took me in. 'What ever you do to the least of my brethren you do it to Me.'

> The fruit of Silence is Prayer
> The fruit of Prayer is Faith
> The fruit of Faith is Love
> The fruit of Love is Service

Pat Arrowsmith

Assistant Editor, Amnesty International
Vice-President, Campaign for Nuclear Disarmament

GOOD GOD

God is good –
sparkled stamen tips,
petal lips
lure insects down
to poison flood,
gorge on
wing filaments,
delicate
long legs.

God is good,
loves blood –
lion tear
deer,
zebra,
bear
to red
shreds;
pussies pounce on
fledglings
mesmerized
to flustered
fear.

God is good,
kind –
men wound fish
for fun,
slice bull
for steak,
skin seal
for coat,
sear bunny-eyes
for hair-spray,
turn dolphin
into missile.

God is good,
is love –
made pearl
of a world,
luminous bubble
to be burst
by worst
of his species:
humans,
who stab,
shock,
strangle,
shoot,

crucify
each other
in this cause
or that;
even scheme
to poison space,
slay
all other creatures,
obliterate
everyone's habitat,
entire planet –
so kind,
so loving,
so good
is God . . .

My hat!

Senator Edward M. Kennedy

I believe in a just and loving God who gives us direction and support.

I believe that there is life after death, and that we are judged. I believe in the Resurrection, in Jesus Christ as the Saviour, and that through His suffering, death, and resurrection we are redeemed and shall be united with him.

As the soul is the life of the body, so God is the life of the soul.
St Augustine

David Alton MP

God is personal to each of us through the presence of Jesus, His son. Some people regard God as a concept – perhaps the force of good or the abstract creator – which all seems unnecessarily academic and remote. If you accept the reality of Jesus, as God made man, abstract concepts become redundant. Jesus, as part of the Trinity, is both God and man and is therefore the perfect blue-print for humanity.

The Apostle Paul says that without the resurrection Christianity would be a fraud. The guarantee of Jesus Christ's own resurrection is that each of us will also rise from the dead. Jesus' own life, death, and life beyond the grave is the confident expectation of all who love Him.

Barbara Cartland

Romantic novelist

WHAT I BELIEVE
One thing, I know, life can never die,
Translucent, splendid, flaming like the sun,
Only our bodies wither and deny
The life-force when our strength is done.

Let me transmit this wonderful fire,
Even a little through my heart and mind,
Bringing the perfect love we all desire
To those who seek, yet blindly cannot find.

We all want to find the World behind the World, we all want to step through the Looking Glass, we all want the security of knowing we are not alone and that death is not the end. It is so easy to say you must have faith but difficult to be sure.

What I do believe, as I have said in my Poem, is that you cannot have death in life – that is impossible – and life is eternal. Only the body, like everything else in nature, when it is old, decays and is thrown away, but the Life-Force within us remains.

What I believe and which has been proved so often in the East, is that in the Wheel of Rebirth we come back with all our good qualities and also our debts to humanity.

There is no other explanation as to why Mozart could play the violin perfectly at the age of four and why a little girl, age three, can play chess with the great experts.

There are innumerable examples of this not only in the past but appearing everyday in the newspapers and it would be an unbelievable waste if the brilliant brain of someone like Winston Churchill, were just lost because we believed he had died.

As Kipling put it so clearly

> They will come back, come back again
> As long as the red earth rolls,
> He never wasted a leaf or tree,
> Do you think He would squander souls?

What is important for all of us, is that we should try and reach the Divine ourselves and actually it is perfectly possible for everyone. We can do this through Concentration, Meditation, Positive Thinking or what has been called for thousands of years – Prayer.

Prayer is not just a begging bowl for our needs, but something far more esoteric and wonderful. It is an uplifting of the heart and spirit and it happens not at specified times that we choose, but a hundred times a day often without our being consciously aware of it.

Every time we feel that quick uplift within us at the sight of beauty, the sound of music or the note of love in someone's voice, that is Prayer and our link with the world beyond this.

Sunshine on still water, the breeze in the trees, leafless branches against a winter's sky and in the passing of the second I feel with them – that is a Prayer.

In the ecstasy that happens between a man and a woman when they really love each other and they 'make love', that is the nearest we get in this dimension to the love of God or the Life-Force, whichever you like to call it.

It is available for everyone and we just have to have the initiative and the commonsense to lift ourselves towards the Infinite.

Kim Casali

'Love is' Cartoonist

God is of course thousands of years old but looks eternally youthful at about 38 years old in earth time. He is of medium height with golden blond curly hair and brown laughing eyes. His face is animated and jovial. He has a distinct aura enveloping Him which draws one to Him but makes one feel very comfortable although in awe of Him. He reflects infinite wisdom, gentleness, humour, dignity and most of all love which He gives to all equally. He has great patience with all of us and does not rush to the aid of any particular individual but gives us the love and courage to help ourselves as the true leader and guide He is.

The soul separates from the lifeless body and we enter a new world whilst still being able to see the earth plane and in fact the body we have just discarded. The kind of person we were and our behaviour on earth towards our fellow man determines what awaits us in death. The spirit or soul lives on and the Heaven which we readily refer to is just the atmosphere all around the earth. Spirit people can see each other and live 'lives' very similar to those on earth but since there is no body to sustain, eating is unnecessary. There are delicious fruits and other tasty morsels to savour but only for pleasure, not sustenance.

Spirit people live in different levels or realms, the lowest and

love is...

...a gift from God - to share.

darkest for those who lived very sinful lives on earth and the highest and brightest for those who have spent their earth and spirit lives devoted to helping and loving one another. God does not condemn us to one realm or another, our attitude does, and the highest realms are within reach of every soul born. We work in the spirit world to benefit other spirits, to gain wisdom, to bring beauty to the spirit world or to help people on earth and also those who have just died and need help in adjusting to a different existence. Those who have died quickly or violently such as in accidents or murders, need help to adjust.

Spirit people talk to one another but their voices are on a frequency unable to be heard by earth people other than those with spiritual gifts, but they also communicate by thoughts.

We grow and develop in the spirit world although we appear to stay looking middle aged even when we are very, very old. Those who have died in infancy or at a young age will grow and mature as they would on earth.

The after-life is not all religion, church and sermons. A wicked and sinful fellow who has spent much of his life on earth doing unjust deeds to his fellow man will not be given absolution because he says, 'God forgive me!' on his death bed. In the after life he will find himself in one of the lower realms where he will have to undergo a complete change of attitude, be truly repentant and work to help others before he can enjoy the serenity that can be found in the after-life.

Derek Bond

Actor

As a Christian I believe in God.

God, as I try to comprehend him, is the sum total of all of us, his creatures, and, indeed, of the entire universe. In a fumbling way I feel that God is made up of all matter known to man in the same way that our human bodies are made up of atoms and molecules.

I believe that this concept is so baffling and difficult for us to comprehend fully that God tried to reach our human consciousness by taking on human form in the person of Jesus Christ.

I believe in an after-life but have no conception of its shape or form. I accept the fact of Resurrection in spirit but not in the flesh. I am content to wait in faith until the ultimate truth is revealed.

One further conviction I have is that our heaven and hell are within us in life. Which one of us has not experienced that moment at a time of personal triumph and euphoria when the memory of some evil deed or act of unkindness we have been guilty of appears like an avenging angel to chasten and humble us?

I believe, too, that our eternity in some small degree is held in the memories of those who have really known us in life — for the good that was in us and, alas, for the evil.

Alan Parker
Film director

•ઙ · ઙ•

I've never been too sure about God. I always knew he was there even though my good Socialist upbringing told me he probably wasn't. After all, if he was, how could he put up with so much inequality, pain and misery in the world? Surely no one as smart as God would allow us to be that stupid? I suppose, I saw God as a sort of Sports Master with a beard and a Cecil B. De Mille video under his arm.

When I was younger it was so much easier. In Islington, where I grew up, the Boys' Brigade had the best football team, swimming team, gymnastic team, etc., etc., and all we had to do to win all those cups was to put up with Bible Class every Sunday for an hour, even though we thought it a bit daft. In those days 'the good book' was the one kept by Lance Corporal Langley on the Harringay dog racing. The assembled yobbos would lustily sing 'Holy Holy Holy' but with an eye on the clock so that we could get to Hackney Marshes on time for Sunday kick-offs. We even slipped in a prayer now and again for a five nil win and more often than not it worked, so who was to say there wasn't a Brian Clough up there in the sky to guide us?

When I got older, frankly, it became more difficult. Maybe he didn't exist at all, and if he did maybe *he* was a *she*. Somehow, there was just too much cruelty around to believe in a benign omnipotence. In a world where Shi-ites, Jews, Catholics and Protestants blew children apart in the name of big G, who could possibly believe? But as the old man said, there's probably just enough religion in the world to make us hate one another, but sadly not enough to make us love. One day maybe.

When you die I think you get to come back again. Probably in the form of something more hideous and more awful than the human mind can possibly imagine. In my case, I'll probably come back as a film critic.

Sir John Mills CBE

When I pray I find, because I have no personal concept of God, that I pray to Jesus who, since my early childhood days, has always seemed very real to me.

I wish that I could visualize God in the same way; it would strengthen my belief in 'a divinity that shapes our ends'.

I am convinced after years of questioning that God exists; each new Spring that I am privileged to see and wonder at strengthens my faith, for this immaculate perfection there can be no other answer.

What happens when I die?

I find that a question difficult to answer because I do not believe in death. My body, brain and mind will, one day, stop functioning, but my spirit, which is me, will continue on its adventure.

I believe I shall be reunited with those I loved during my time on this planet.

An old mystic says somewhere, 'God is an unutterable sigh in the innermost depths of the soul.' With still greater justice, we may reverse the proposition, and say the soul is a never ending sigh after God.

Theodor Christlieb

Peter Cushing

Actor

◦§ · ≽◦

How can I answer such imponderables, I thought, chewing the end of my pencil. My beliefs are simple and as firm as a rock, but not easy to put on paper. However, I must try.

Let's take the 'Who' in the first question – that's simple enough; my late beloved wife Helen, because she was (and still is, for that matter) the personification of all that is Good; you only have to substract an 'o' from the adjective, and you have God. *Goodness*.

Now to the 'What'. I looked up the word 'manifest' in my copy of Chambers, and this is what I read: '. . . that may be easily seen by the eye or perceived by the mind; . . . to put beyond doubt; to reveal or declare . . .' So – He *manifests* Himself by all the beauty that surrounds us, even in the sometimes 'ugly' world of today. Just look at the stars, so ordered and so steadfast and so important (to sailors, for instance) and – *so beautiful*; observe the beauty of all the flora and fauna which abounds about us, everything put on this earth for specific purposes. Who by? God, of course. I'm afraid familiarity has bred a certain contempt, because many people take too much for granted and do not realize that He reveals His message in such an uncomplicated way by the Seasons. Spring brings birth and life, Summer fulfilment, Autumn tranquillity and Winter the peaceful rest of death; but what happens next year – and the next? The same cycle, demonstrating His assurance of life eternal for *all* His creations, the most important being mankind. With all our faults, we've been blessed with brains capable of doing wondrous things, which leads me into answering the second question – 'What happens when we die?'

What a waste if all the knowledge accrued during our three-score-year-and-ten cannot be put to some good use in some other place at some other time! Our given period on *this* earth is like being in kindergarten, during which we better ourselves for the promised paradise, where we will be reunited with our loved ones who have already reached those 'many mansions'. ('Eye hath not seen nor ear heard the things God hath prepared . . . He shall wipe away every tear from our eyes. There shall be no more death, no mourning nor crying nor pain any more, for the old bad things will have passed away . . .')

Sitting around on clouds all day just twanging a harp is not my idea of Heaven. I reckon we'll be as busy up there as we have been down here, but in an even *more* beautiful place!

So there we are – and I leave you with the words of the popular song which Dame Vera Lynn used to sing; 'I'll be seeing you in all the old familiar places . . .' – just you wait and see!

Michael Winner

Film director

Most of the time I find it difficult to believe that any God could permit so many other people in this world to lead the lives that are put upon them. Therefore I doubt His existence. However, when my own life takes a turn for the worse I give Him the benefit of the doubt and assume He might be there and turn to Him, greedily, for help and assistance.

I think that I go to a wonderful tea party in the sky, set in an English garden, and alternately set in other beautiful places – with excellent company and very good cream cakes. Somewhere below, visible as if in a small pond, in a place less pleasant, are those of whom I disapprove suffering dreadfully.

God is not the name of God, but an opinion about Him.
Pope Xystus I

Jeremy Irons
Actor

I believe God is the force for good in the world and in each individual and may be used or not. This, of course, makes the devil a force for evil.

I remain unsure what happens when we die, though I suspect – as physicists tell me that energy cannot be destroyed – that what is known as the 'after life' is the force for good or evil that has rubbed off us on to other people, and things, during our lives.

Rabbi Julia Neuberger

For me God is almost impossible to describe. Sometimes I feel the attempt is arrogant. Sometimes I feel God is so other, so different, from human beings, that there are no words available. Sometimes I feel God is a creative force, a dynamic in the universe, which starts us off but gives us free will, and therefore again is not amenable to our examination.

But there are other times I feel God very near to me. He, she or it is still indescribable, but there is a being, a force, a spirit with which I have a tenuous relationship some of the time, and a closer one the rest. Sometimes I talk to it. Sometimes I feel I hear, or sense, a reply. But that answer comes from within me, a voice of conscience, which may be the nearest we get to hearing God's voice, even though we cannot be sure that that is what it is. Yet there is a sense of a presence, a still small voice, an awareness of something both within and beyond us, which for me is what God is.

But if you ask me what I believe will happen when we die, I have to say that personally I think it is probably nothing. One cannot tell, and it seems to me that speculation is pointless, but one must live as if this life is the only one we have – and, should there be another, then that will be a bonus. Most Jews, particularly orthodox Jews, would not be as adamant as I am in this regard. But Judaism does stress 'this life' beyond any other possibilities, and we know that in this life we can affect what happens to ourselves and others. So this life is what we should stress. No other.

R. Graham Phaup

District Manager, Christian Science Committees on
Publication for Great Britain and Ireland

⋅⋅⋅

The Bible tells us that God is Love and this is my highest concept
of Him. I think of God as entirely good, infinitely strong and
tender – a loving and caring Father-Mother, who cherishes and
nurtures His children. I believe this loving bond between the
Father and His universal family is unbreakable throughout
eternity. Even a glimpse of His ever-presence – full of light and
glory – fills me with awe and wonder.

I think of God also as infinite Spirit, the perfect creator of a
perfect, spiritual universe, including man in His image and
likeness, which forever expresses His own nature. I believe that
God's will for man is good, always for innocence, wholeness and
freedom. The material, mortal man and the universe which
appear to the physical senses – with all the sin, disease and
misery they include – I see as limited and mistaken concepts of
God's creation which need to be outgrown through spiritual
rebirth and regeneration.

It's evident that a completely good God never created evil, and
I see this as the basis for challenging and overcoming the evils we
encounter in the world. The light of God's presence dispels the
darkness and His saving grace offers redemption to humanity,
lifting us out of the depths of ignorance, sin and suffering and
restoring us to our natural state of purity and innocence.

Through prayer, we can all commune with God – hear His
voice and increasingly bring our thoughts and lives into obedience
to Him. The Bible is of priceless value in enabling us to draw
closer to God. The Scriptures teach us who we are and how we
should live. I look especially to Jesus Christ as the Son of God and
the Saviour of the world, whose life and healing ministry,
redeeming the sinner, restoring the sick and bringing joy to
human existence, has opened up a radically different way of living.

Jesus taught us to love God supremely and our neighbour as

ourselves. I believe that through studying his teachings and striving to follow his example, we can increasingly recognize our eternal relationship to God as His beloved children, and feel His love and power in our lives.

Through his resurrection, Jesus triumphed over death and proved that life goes on even after the physical senses declare that it is over.

A boat might sail out of sight over the horizon and an observer on the shore could mistakenly believe that the boat had ceased to exist. I think death is something like this. We no longer see a friend, and lament his passing. But it is simply the entrance into a different stage of existence, in which he will continue with conscious identity as before. I do not believe people immediately attain the kingdom of heaven as a result of that experience, but rather that after it, they go on learning and growing spiritually until they reach the full consciousness of their eternal identity as God's beloved children.

Maureen Lipman
Actress and author

I have several concepts of God. One is William Blake-like – an angry, fiery, billowy figure on a cloud pointing an accusing finger down AT ME!

The other is of a whacky sort of script editor-cum-producer of a very long-running soap opera, sitting round a table with a lot of bored angels: Shakespeare, Wilde, Shaw, Tolstoy and Lenny Bruce – playing with executive toys and saying things like: 'How about a new story-line for the Rosenthal family? Things have been going a bit too smoothly of late, haven't they . . . ?'

In answer to what I think happens when we die – I'd like to think that we just kind of change channels; in other words, we leave this programme and this entity – look down on it and see how trite it really was, and have another try somewhere else. But I hope, unlike most actors, there's a good long period of resting in between. If there's a judgement day, I've had it!!

Jilly Cooper
Author and journalist

✍ · ঌ

My grandmother had a good concept of God, in which she said she was a grain of sand in a vat of water and God was the water all around her. I am not sure I believe that but I know, shamingly, I believe in God a lot more when I am in trouble (which is quite often). I do think prayer works. I like to hope that when I die I will get to heaven in the end, because I would like to see my father and all my dogs again. But I don't have very high hopes.

Jane Asher
Actress and author

I only wish I did have a clear concept of God. All I can think is that it is something far more complicated and hard to understand than my poor brain can grasp at this stage, but I certainly have the feeling that there is some deep mystery behind this extraordinary existence.

I suspect that when I die, I shall feel exactly as I did in 1542. By that I am afraid I don't mean that I believe in reincarnation, but that I suspect a total blank. I very much hope that I shall be proved wrong.

Mary Whitehouse CBE

President, National Viewers' and Listeners' Association

My God is a very personal one. The words I most often say to myself, especially at times when I face difficulties and trials, are these – 'He walks with me and He talks with me and He tells me that I am His own.' I believe that God guides in the simplest as well as the most important decisions we have to make and that He often does so through quite unexpected channels.

I find immense spiritual sustenance and peace in the wonders and beauty of nature, particularly in the soil, the flowers and the trees of our own garden.

What do I believe happens when I die? To tell the truth this is something that I think about hardly at all. I just feel content to leave it all in His hands and try to make the most of being alive! Though I do have a deep sense that all will be well.

Jane Lapotaire

Actress

'God is that unfathomable something in us and all around us which is not ourselves.'

When I die I hope to encounter that Light and Energy which reaffirm their presence, and continually elude me but for which my journey on this earth is a permanent search.

Yoko Ono

God is the unknown power which is within us.

Death is a transition.

Annie Lennox

Singer and songwriter

It's a tricky subject, as I've never had any firm beliefs. Perhaps it would be fair to say that we've been introduced several times but I've never actually made his acquaintance.

God perplexes me. There are too many associations with too many things that I cannot get to grips with. When I discuss the subject with people who claim to 'know' I usually discover a fixed belief system which is too unnaturally palatable for me to feel comfortable with.

I suspect life could be a lot simpler if I could accept what people tell me (with such authority). But who are you supposed to believe when there are hundreds of different faiths, doctrines and interpretations of so many 'holy books'?

As I write I find myself falling into the perfect trap of setting myself up for a good old religious argument. And the more I write the more I realize that the entire subject makes me highly suspicious.

So God stays 'up there' and I for my part stay 'down here', curiously waiting to see if I ever do make a more intimate acquaintance.

Lulu

Singer

I don't actually think of God as being a man, a physical being, but as something that is all around us, within each and every one of us. I pray to God. I try to bring out the good and positive side of myself which is also God and I try to see it in anybody and everybody else. In this way I try to do the best with my life and see the best in everybody else. This I believe makes a person positive and happy. Maybe not all the time, but who knows – maybe eventually I will reach that stage!

I believe that when I die my spiritual body leaves my physical body and moves on to another plane, and I think there are many different planes. But believing as I do I am therefore not afraid to die.

Mahārāṇī dāsī (Poly Styrene)

Singer and songwriter

My concept of God is not my own mental concoction, but one that has been passed down through a disciplic succession of spiritual teachers according to the Vedic tradition.

One of the loveliest descriptions of God that I have come across is in the Brahma-saṁhitā *Hymns of Brahmā*. Brahmā meditated upon Lord Sri Krishna and the Brahma-saṁhitā is the expression of Brahmā's vision of the spiritual realm.

veṇuṁ kvaṇantam aravinda-dalāyatākṣaṁ
barhāvataṁsam asitāmbuda-sundarāṅgam
kandarpa-koṭi-kamanīya-viśeṣa-śobhaṁ
govindam ādi-puruṣaṁ tam ahaṁ bhajāmi

Text 30

Translation by His Divine Grace Bhaktisiddhānta Sarasvatī Goswami Ṭhākura:

I worship Govinda, the primeval Lord, who is adept in playing on His flute, with blooming eyes like lotus petals, with head decked with peacock's feather, with the figure of beauty tinged with the hue of blue clouds, and His unique loveliness charming millions of Cupids.

With such blissful revelations as these who could fail to adore the supreme personality of Godhead Sri Krishna?

At the time of death if my life has been spiritually successful by faithfully and sincerely rendering service to Krishna I will attain a spiritual body befitting my relationship with God where I will continue to serve the all-attractive Lord Sri Krishna and His associates in the spiritual realm. Although I do not especially desire this privilege it is the birthright of the human form of life and is the result of devotional service.

Gaily I lived, as ease and nature taught,
And spent my little life without a thought;
And am amazed that Death, that tyrant grim,
Should think of me, who never thought of him.

Anonymous, *Epitaph*

64

Dame Iris Murdoch CBE
Novelist and philosopher

I do not believe in a personal God, and as 'God' seems to name a supernatural person I avoid the word. I do not believe in the divinity of Christ or in any place, such as 'heaven', which is in any literal sense outside our world. However, I believe in religion, in a spiritual realty which can transform our being, leading us away from the false unreal 'goods' of the selfish ego, towards what is really good. This might be called a kind of Platoism, which for me remains very close to the wisdom of Christianity, as expressed for instance by St Augustine.

I do not believe in an after-life or in any form of reincarnation. Religion, the struggle between good and evil, and appearance and reality, it is every moment here and now.

Mary Hayley Bell
Playwright, poet and author

God Almighty Maker of Heaven and Earth – the great Spirit to me as an individual is quite simply a Higher Power, not in the way some formal Church tradition or TV preacher may picture Him – He is a Force, an Energy, or concept that is outside ourselves, stronger than ourselves, more powerful than ourselves.

I believe when I die that my spirit cannot be destroyed, and when my physical body falls into its deep sleep, it merely leaves its 'overcoat' behind and joins those spirits which have gone before, the ones we have loved who are always with us, guarding and guiding.

I believe too that I have been here before and will return again. I believe that Love is stronger than Death and I will never be separated from those I love.

Thora Hird OBE
Actress

◆§ · ℰ◆

I was born in Morecambe – a seaside town in Lancashire. My grandfather and my uncles – on my mother's side, were fishermen who trawled for the famous Morecambe Bay Shrimps. They all wore navy blue woollen guernsey (jerseys) and most of them had beards. Uncle Robert was in our house one morning and a neighbour, who had nipped in for something or other, said to him, 'See, Robert you do look like Jesus!' She said this quite seriously and sincerely. I was about four or five years old and I can remember – vividly – looking at the kind eyes, bearded face and jet black hair that curled out from under his cap and thinking – 'Yes – he does look like all the pictures I've seen of Jesus'. Consequently, from then on not only was I convinced in my young mind that Uncle Robert looked like Jesus but that Jesus looked like Uncle Robert.

Each night as I said my prayers – 'Gentle Jesus, meek and mild . . .' I said the prayer to a Jesus in a navy blue woollen fisherman's guernsey and a cap – I was so sure Jesus looked like Uncle Robert.

When I was ten years old – well acquainted with Sunday School and Chapel, it began to dawn on me that perhaps Jesus didn't really look like Uncle Robert or Uncle Robert like Jesus. One night, when my mother was sitting on the side of my bed whilst I said my prayers, I said to her, rather sadly, 'Jesus doesn't really look like Uncle Robert – does he?' As I knelt there in my pyjamas (that had been warmed in the oven next to the fire) and my hair in curlrags, she cupped my chin with her hand, looked me in the eyes – so very lovingly, and said, 'Who says he doesn't?' I've thought of that moment, with great affection, so very often because in my opinion the Lord looks as we want him to look.

So often I am asked 'When did you find out there is a God?' I always answer truthfully, 'I never knew a time when he wasn't there!'

I know what I *hope* happens – that my loved ones will be awaiting me with open arms and that in time *I* can await other loved ones who still have their spell of life on this earth. I cannot believe there is 'nothing' after our wonderful life here – however, like everyone else, I shall find out when the time comes – and may I be prepared for whatever the Good Lord decides.

Margaret, Duchess of Argyll
Novelist

By my upbringing and by instinct I have always believed that God exists.

However, having seen and read of the cruelty to old women, babies and animals every year I am beginning to wonder.

As I feel strongly that my father is ever present and helping me, I have no doubt that the dead are in contact with the living.

God and other artists are always a little obscure.
Oscar Wilde

Sylvia Syms
Actress

I have no concept of God as something or somebody separate. What I see in my fellow human beings seems to encompass everything from the concept of absolute good to total evil. People are capable of such a variety of actions, thoughts and creations that to conceive of anything wider in scope is not possible for me. 'God' is in us all.

Nothing, except that the body rots and can help to fertilize the earth – ashes certainly make good compost. My idea of immortality would be a kind thought from somebody – or one of my children telling one of their children 'My mum used to do or say so-and-so . . .' It will not last long, but it is enough.

Cleo Laine OBE
Singer

I have always been aware of something bigger out there in the big wide world – something unexplainable – something deep inside oneself that moves you and nature. If one needs to put a name to it then, yes, call that unexplainable feeling God.

I have no idea how to answer the second question. It's a complete mystery to everyone, I think. But I'd like to come back and haunt a few people!

Loretta Young

Actress

My beloved God is 'the creator' of all. He had no beginning and He will have no end.

His teaching (the Bible) is for me the perfect 'how to' book, for all mankind, for each and every individual on the face of this earth.

He is my father, my lover, my protector, my judge, without whom I could not exist nor would I wish to.

I shall go directly to my Lord, to be judged. As I will still be imperfect (as all humans are) I shall spend an allotted time in purgatory, in reparation for my sins.

Then eventually, according to God's plan, I will spend eternity in the arms of my lover – my beloved God, the creator of heaven and earth.

All this if I am true to Him, now.

The more I learn of Him, the more I think of Him, the more I love Him, lean on Him, and live for Him.

He is indeed the food of my life – my real life in Him and – I believe this tremendous lover of mine – will be anyone's – He has said so.

Dr Billy Graham

Christian Evangelist

God is the Creator of everything in the universe – including each one of us. Not only is He our Creator, but He loves us and wants to be our Father as well. Although He created man with a free will, man used that free will to disobey and turn away from God, and as a result man is now alienated from God and His blessings. But instead of destroying man (as He had every right to do), God sent His only Son, Jesus Christ, to take the punishment we deserved so we could be forgiven and reconciled to HIM. By committing ourselves to Christ by faith, we can become God's children and know Christ as our Redeemer, friend, and guide to everlasting life.

When I die the Scriptures teach I will be at home with God forever, along with the many loved ones from all over the world who have trusted Christ and have preceded me.

Bapak Muhammad Subuh Sumohadiwidjojo (1901–1987)
Javanese Muslim, Founder and Spiritual Guide of Subud

God cannot be described. If you wish to know what God looks like, you must first know what everything in the universe looks like. It can be said that He is like a tornado. It can also be said that He is like thunder. Why is this? It is because God is Almighty and envelops the whole universe. So do not have far reaching thoughts about where and how God is, whether God has a beard or a moustache. Don't. It is not possible. Just feel what envelops you inside and outside. Later on you will eventually know. You will not know how God is in a definite form, but you will know his Power which is with you and within you.

Truly we cannot know God, for God is not of a kind we can know. Could we know God He would be ordinary. But on the other hand God knows us. God knows man's condition, his mind, his heart, his feelings and his imagination and everything needed for his life in this world. God knows these things.

God is always with you. God envelops you inwardly and outwardly. God is actually nearer than your sight when you are looking at something, nearer than your thoughts when you are thinking. But if man wishes to go towards God, then He is far, far away; so that the distance cannot be measured. Therefore it is not possible for man to come into the presence of God unless it is His will.

When we die, all our knowledge, all our thinking, all our feelings, everything we have been attached to in this world disappear completely. We are at that moment in a state of complete darkness – there is nothing left of all we had in this world. And God has said: in that moment I will guide you . . . The power of God will be there at the last moment when you face death and everything has been taken away from you.

When you finally face death with the passions stopped, the thinking stopped, and your everyday understanding stopped, there will arise an enlightenment, a vast understanding that cannot be known by people living in this world . . . The Messengers of God have explained that conditions in the life after death are far more glorious and enduring than in this one. Our present life can be compared to an overnight stop, whereas afterwards the time is immeasureable. Once you have experienced the other worlds beyond this one, then this world is nothing and there seems no reason to live here. Therefore pray to God that you will find your way there in your life after death, and that you will be able to work in that world, a world far more glorious than this, the world that is truly heaven.

Death is the great adventure, beside which moonlandings and space trips pale into insignificance.

Joseph Bayly

'So far it's been downhill all the way . . .'

Charlton Heston

Actor

Who or what is your personal concept of God?

I go with Carlyle here. He said, 'I don't pretend to understand the universe – it's a great deal bigger than I am . . .' I'm personally inclined to the conviction that there must be Some-body out there.

What do you believe happens to you when you die?

I have no idea. Obviously, like all the rest of us, I will find out.

Robin Knox-Johnston CBE, RD
Round-the-world yachtsman

Who is God?
The person I talk to is, probably because of early influences in my life, a rather kindly, retired, Sea Captain.
What is God?
The human personification of the natural laws that govern us. This is putting it terribly simply. Whereas it is quite easy to grasp the concept of say, meteorology, it is almost impossible to grasp the concept of an infinite universe, governed by laws that we still do not understand. It is possible, however, for we humans to grasp the concept of some super human being who does understand it all.

I hope that all the people who have talked about a Heaven we go to after we die are right. It makes the fading visions of immortality which come as one gets older, easier to bear! I will look forward to seeing all my friends and relations again, and being able to talk to people who I have missed by years on earth. This assumes, of course, that I have managed to persuade the judges responsible that the life I have led here is reasonably in accordance with a Christian philosophy.

God is truth, and light His shadow.
Plato

Sir Robert Armstrong GCB, CVO
Former Secretary of the Cabinet and Head of the Home Civil Service

I can only say that my beliefs on these matters are derived from detailed study of the Gospels and of the Acts of the Apostles when I was at school, and are basically in conformity with the doctrines of the Church of England.

Admiral of the Fleet Sir John Fieldhouse
GCB, GBE
Chief of the Defence Staff

1. In military terms 'the everlasting and everloving Commander-in-Chief who ordered and organized this marvellous Universe.'

2. I don't know but I *believe* I shall find out and am not worried by that prospect.

Ron Todd
General Secretary, Transport and General Workers Union

I grew up in a London market environment in which a multi-cultured population worshipped many Gods, within the group of Jewish, Catholic and Moslem races.

My own concept of God is of an all powerful spirit conceived in the minds of those across the centuries who sought reassurance that life was pre-ordained and would continue in Valhalla, the happy hunting ground, or with illustrious ancestors.

That belief and faith I envy but I believe that with death comes extinction.

Lech Walesa

Chairman, the National Commission of Solidarity

This is not the kind of question I could answer in one sentence – and I have no time for more elaborate replies.

So long as we live we shall never learn what happens after man dies – this is a mystery. But we trust in God and He gives us the grace of life after death.

Bert Kitchen

Artist and cartoonist

The image came to me first before its significance.

I think the Crown of thorns symbolizes for me: the cruelty of man; the destructive side of man and Death.

The Rose – the good that survives in spite of the Crown.

So I suppose – the Crown – Death and the Rose – Life.

The Crown could not be portrayed in a gentle manner mainly because I am bitterly disappointed in the amount of cruelty that exists in the world, which becomes more apparent as time passes.

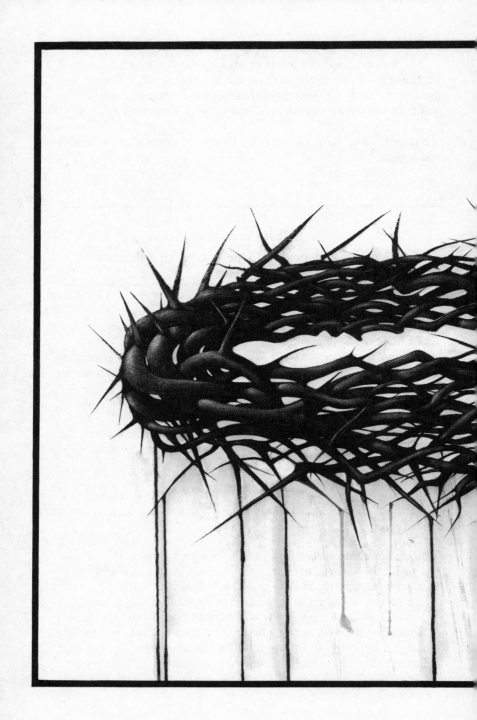

Richard Adams
Novelist

·ᘐ · ᘗ·

My answer to your two questions is that the answers are to be found in the Gospels. It is impossible for a human being to conceive of God, but through His grace we are enabled to conceive of Him through the human personality of Our Lord. As to what happens when you die, Our Lord has told us all that is necessary for us to know during this life. If we needed to know any more, He would have told us.

My general view about subjects of this nature is that it is a great pity that so many people nowadays do not seem to read the Gospels or to place reliance upon them as a source of revealed truth.

Rev. Bernard Thorogood
General Secretary, The United Reformed Church

·ᘐ · ᘗ·

A host of images is needed for us to attempt any concept of God and the Bible is full of them. Some now seem less helpful – such as the aloof judge and the military commander. Some grow on us as we make our pilgrimage. Here are three personal images.

God the Composer, who has written the most glorious music of creation, and who sees it murdered by the inefficient, squabbling orchestra in which the players ignore each other and struggle to come out on top. Yet the underlying music is there if only we listen for it and offer our talents to play it.

God the Lover, who longs for all that is best for us, who knows us as we are, who plunges into life to be with us, who sheds blood for us and yet who loves us enough to let us choose our own path.

God the Centre – of the universe, at rest amid the moving stars; – of the world, around whom the nations spin; – of my life, even when thought and action carry me far from the holy light and truth; always the point of return.

I believe that our visible life is rather like the womb from which we will be born. We cannot see beyond it or have any concept of that further life. We can only have clues from the best of what this narrower life brings to us. Beauty and maturity, wisdom and honesty, compassion and steadfastness – these are glimpses of God's presence which we have seen in Jesus, and which will not be ended when we lay aside the flesh we see and touch.

Sir *Colin* Davis CBE

God is everything I do not understand and also the energy with which I try to understand a little more.

We all know what happens to the body when we die and I must needs believe it. What happens to the energy, just supposing there is any left, is anybody's guess.

At last I heard a voice upon the slope
Cry to the summit, 'Is there any hope?'
To which an answer pealed from that high land,
But in a tongue no man could understand;
And on the glimmering limit far withdrawn,
God made Himself an awful rose of dawn.
                    Alfred Lord Tennyson

Paul McCartney MBE
Singer and songwriter

❧ · ❧

God is a shortened version of good.

In the words of John Le Mesurier – When you die you conk out!

Paul Weller
Singer and songwriter

❧ · ❧

God is the creator of this beautiful Earth, all that we need and may ever need is contained here, we have no need to look into space or beyond, we couldn't hope to find anything better.

That there are so many greedy people amongst us is not a fault of God but of man and his fundamental capitalism. Because of that we may or may not suffer forever. That's not the way it was planned but the way mankind has designed it. God was/is a socialist.

Your spirit is preserved in a memory, your actions on Earth define this. Ghosts are spirits who people have forgotten about . . . so do what you can now.

❧ · ❧

When a man dies he clutches in his hands only that which he has given away in his lifetime.   – Jean-Jacques Rousseau

Lionel Jeffries
Actor

◆§ · ह●

This is a true story. In a circuitous way it answers both your questions – I think.

My Uncle Fred was a dear, and I loved him. He was, however, the most bigoted of men. He quite simply detested all Catholics, Jews, and any member of the human race who was darker, or yellower, than the true white, Anglo Saxon, Protestant resident of Herne Hill.

I visited him on the Thursday afternoon. Auntie Lily had telephoned to say that he was 'on his way out', and possibly had 'till Friday before he shuffled off his mortal 'thingymebob'.

'What do you think God will look like Uncle?'

'I'll let you know, boy,' he whispered. 'I should be seeing Him come Saturday.'

'You're going to get the shock of your death if He turns out to be black, Jewish, and part-time Catholic.'

'If He is, I ain't bloody staying.'

He winked, smiled, and closed his tired, old, blue eyes.

Sure enough, Saturday morning, six thirty, he 'blew it' for good.

That was eight years ago.

I've not heard from him since. Whatever God was like He obviously suited Uncle Fred, and Uncle Fred, I suppose, by the same token, suited God.

I trust it's going to be the same for me, and you – God willing.

◆§ · ह●

Amid so much war and contest and variety of opinion, you will find one consenting conviction in every land, that there is one God, the King and Father of all. — Maximus Tyrius

Swami Bhavyananda

Spiritual leader, the Ramakrishna Vedanta Centre

◄§ · §►

We human beings caught up in the turmoil of life feel lost. We normally take the challenge of life in our stride and successfully deal with it, but sometimes our abilities prove to be futile. Our plans seemed perfect, our execution faultless and still the whole thing failed. But why? There seems to be some unseen factor coming into play in all our activities. Often, we cannot put our finger on it. All the same, it is there. For want of a better word we call it God.

Is this 'God' personal, impersonal or beyond both? For me, God is the creative Power behind this whole universe. It is not only a creation, but also the preservation and destruction of this created universe. If He is the all-pervading Power, He cannot be personal, nor can He be located in any particular point in space and time. My God is One who is intimately connected with this universe. He interpenetrates and is immanent in it. Impelled by that Power, the universe works and operates. Nothing can happen without Him. Even in destruction it is the power of God that functions. God is nature. The power we see in nature is God alone.

When the human mind cannot grasp the impersonal expression of this creative power (God), it tends to personalize it. At our stage of existence we can experience this God only through our senses. They can appreciate only a name and form; they are created that way; so, to meet my personal requirement, I think of God with a name and form, full of virtues, who will be a source of inspiration for me to raise myself above myself.

God as an immanent power is present in everything in this universe. There is nothing inanimate in creation. God is referred to in the Hindu concept as Satchidananda: Existence, Knowledge and Bliss. At one level, life and consciousness are perceived. At the human level, an additional dimension of Self-awareness manifests. When the highest degree of this perfection is reached, there is no difference between God and man. When this distinction is lost, the mortal becomes immortal. That is the goal of human life, towards which we are all progressing. The difference between the creature and the Creator disappears and the Creator alone remains. That is what God is.

Birth and death are part of the flow of things. The individual soul, even before it reaches the human body, has assumed other bodies and cast them off. At the human level itself, the divine, though it has reached a level of self-consciousness, is still far from full manifestation. Religious disciplines are a way of reaching the higher destiny of man. At one end of this voyage of discovery man is very nearly an animal; at the other end he is a saint, very nearly God.

God seems to demand of human beings who are in a higher stage of evolution some effort to meet Him. Man is consciously or unconsciously seeking the Reality inherent in him. Human history is full of people who are in quest of Reality. The span of human life is too short to bring about this complete transformation. Depending on how we have used the opportunities of life and the effort we have put in the right direction, we come back to this terrestrial realm to continue our journey to meet the Creator. Until we reach the unity of life, we shall have many opportunities and chances to achieve this goal. Until we reach the end of our journey, we are subject to the law of cause and effect. The pace of our progress is determined by our desires and actions. Our present is conditioned by our past, and what we do now will determine our future. Death and rebirth do not interrupt this process. We are responsible for our present condition. We can mould our future with courage and determination. With healthy attitudes, inner betterment is achieved. Man has freedom to do this. This freedom itself is something beyond nature. There is a moral order in the world making each man responsible for his deeds. His insight and character grow steadily until he attains perfection. Rebirth means the doctrine of succession of opportunities for improving our knowledge and character. God and the human soul are not different. With the help of reasoning, meditation and contemplation we can achieve this unity. Every lifetime is an opportunity to increase the manifestation of God-consciousness.

Is there an interim period between death and rebirth? It could be anybody's guess. The only lapse of time between death and birth is that which is required to find a suitable family for rebirth. This period may be longer or shorter; sooner or later one is reborn to continue one's journey. As a person grows in his spiritual dimension, all other faculties like aesthetic creativity, ethical sense and love and compassion blossom. Spiritual development is a fulfilment of psychological development. This brings harmony and concord into human life.

Sir Ranulph Fiennes
Explorer

My personal concept of God is that of his son Jesus – who, being a normal sort of bloke, is easy to picture in my mind. Since he was extremely strong willed and withstood even the temptation of avoiding the agony of crucifixion, he helps me to try to face up to my own temptations, such as fear and greed, by thinking back to him, by invoking his great memory.

When I die I think I (minus body) will continue to exist in a more happy world where malice is no longer present between me and the others (in the rest of erstwhile mankind).

You who come my grave to view,
A moment stop and think,
That I am in eternity,
And you are on the brink.
Anonymous, *Epitaph*

Lord John Hunt KG, CBE, DSO
Explorer

For many years I have been disillusioned by organized religion within the Church, to whose dogmas and practices I was expected to adhere from my childhood days. Worship, as a token of personal humility, is a virtue which I acknowledge; I have an abiding sense of wonder at the creation of this planet in the vastness of the Universe. But this is not how I feel about God. For me, God is here among us. I accept God as being a supreme force whose power is Love: love in all its true manifestations.

To try to practise true love is to reach out towards God. To reach that goal of perfect love may be an unattainable human desire; but in every generation there are some people who have progressed a long way towards it. During my life I have been fortunate to meet a few of these rare individuals, whose goodness – or godliness – shines from them.

So I believe that God is Love; this is what Jesus taught his disciples; this was the burden of his sermon on the mountain. I believe that goodness, in however small a measure, is to be found in every human being; that the spark of divinity is within us all. However dimly and even indiscernibly it may burn, it is there and it can be kindled.

When I think of love, I acknowledge its link with, and supremacy over, the other human virtues: for instance humility, selflessness, patience and mercy and certain kinds of courage. These are all expressions of love. From this perspective, the kingdom of God is here on earth, within ourselves. François Varillon in his book *Joie de Croire, Joie de Vivre* expresses this belief far better than I could hope to do.

Of course, I acknowledge the opposite force of Evil: a power opposed to goodness, whose attractions provide us with a choice, so tellingly illustrated in C. S. Lewis' *Screw-Tape Letters*. I am in no doubt about the direction in which lies happiness; but I do not think that the triumph of good over evil can be taken for granted;

in the short term, at least, there are too many pointers in the opposite direction.

You ask me about the 'hereafter'. For me, it is enough to try, with many failings, to practise Jesus' injunction to love other people in my life-time, without being troubled about what lies beyond life. I do not believe our purpose here on earth should be to earn a place in heaven. But I believe there must be some kind of continuity; some continuum of the spirit which links all humanity and which is not severed by death. In a spiritual sense the human concept of time has no meaning. Past, present and future are as one. Difficult though I find it to comprehend, I can accept that it is in this state of timelessness that the spirit within us lives on in the hereafter.

Stirling Moss OBE
Racing driver

I believe in God, but see Him as being the guide of my conscience. I suppose, really, that I see God as the good and kind things that I was taught, mainly by my father and mother, during my up-bringing.

I don't know. I suppose if I really *need* to give an answer, I see it as a continuation of life, where one will meet one's friends, explain one's reasons and make good one's debts.

It is death which gives gambling and heroism their true meaning.
                                                            Albert Camus

Bobby Robson
Manager, English national football team

❧ · ❧

In my view there is a God who, by and large, looks after the human race and attempts to work good in the world. I believe also, however, that there is evil at work in the world and that God is not able on his own to totally counter this. Without this basic belief, I find myself unable to explain some of the terrible things that happen such as natural disasters or the wholescale slaughtering of innocent people by individuals such as Michael Ryan.

I do not believe that there is an after-life. If I can use a cricketing analogy, which is perhaps inappropriate for a football manager, you have one innings. You are in once and out once and that is it.

Fatima Whitbread MBE

Olympic javelin thrower

I believe that he has looked after me in his own special way, only allowing me to succeed when he feels that the time is right.

I am certain that we have been on this earth before in some shape or form and that we will all eventually return in the future with a different identity.

Michael Rogers

Paraplegic author

From the moment of conception, the creation of new life, the division and multiplication of cells to form what we recognize as a 'being', is within itself a physiological and biological miracle. This gift of life is extremely precious, and when combined with perfect health it should be cherished beyond all else.

> When I was a child, I spoke as a child, I thought as a child, my outlook was of a child. But when I became a man, I put away childish things.
>
> (1 Corinthians 13)

I was brought up in the Church of England, and as a young child my concept of God was simple and uncomplicated. It was written that 'God made man in his own image.' I therefore believed God to be of the flesh – a real person – who lived in a mystical place called heaven. I was taught to pray, as most children are, to thank God for the good things in life – the four seasons, the harvest, the sunshine, the trees and flowers, the birds and animals. To look after mummy and daddy, my brother, uncles and aunts. I would also pray for daddy to come home safely from the war. Yet there was no mention of the heinous atrocities of war; of rape and murder; the brutal sexual attacks on women and children; the mugging of the elderly; the abuse of drugs; of the starving; of vice and corruption; of man's inhumanity to man; of disease, disability and death. As I have grown older, and I hope wiser, I have seen and experienced something of the world's suffering and as a result of this I am constantly asking myself 'Why?'

If God created man in his own image, and one must assume God is all good, then why did he create such a magnitude of sin and suffering perpetrated by man? Should God ever appear on earth in person, then surely he must be made answerable for the wilful destruction of this planet by his own creation – man?

Today I describe myself as an agnostic member of the Church of England, for I cannot perceive Christian answers to so much cruelty and injustice in life. I console myself in the belief that life must be like a game of roulette. From the moment of conception, somewhere in planetary space a giant wheel of fortune begins to spin its intricate web of intrigue over our destiny. Some bets we win, others we lose. But for everyone, zero will ultimately come up – some people call this 'Fate'.

If there is a God, then he must be part of us. For me he exists in the wonder of nature, in the birds that return to our shores year after year, in the animals that inhabit our land, in the sunlight, the trees and flowers, the beauty of the countryside, the lakes and rivers, the mountains and valleys, in the innocence of children.

What happens to us when we die? Nobody can truthfully stand up in a Court of Law and swear to reincarnation. It would be wonderful to *know* we would be re-born in another and perhaps better world to continue with work we started during our short lives on this planet. Perhaps the nearest one can get to discovering this answer is to be on the verge of death and resuscitated. This has happened to me eight or more times when I experienced respiratory arrests. I stopped breathing, my heart stopped and I was rendered unconscious. On each occasion I perceived a similar vision. During the first, I visualized myself strapped to the floor of a railway truck descending at great speed down a steep incline that disappeared into a darkened tunnel that led to the bowels of the earth. At the end of the tunnel stood a wall of fire. I instinctively knew – to pass through this wall of fire would lead to death. But the truck stopped just within feet of my doom and slowly reversed up the incline until I found daylight and regained consciousness. On other occasions I visualized myself running with tremendous physical difficulty away from a ball of fire. Again I knew that should I fail to find the energy to keep going, I would be engulfed by the flames and would die. My legs were like lead weights, but slowly I managed to run further and further away from the fire, when I finally regained consciousness.

There are obviously scientific explanations to much of what I experienced. The balls of fire represented the electric light above my bed – the last thing I saw before unconsciousness. The reversal of the railway truck and my running from the fire was the effect of recovery drugs that were being pumped into me. The dead-weight of my legs represented my newly acquired paralysis. Yet the whole experience was literally a nightmare and quite terrifying. There was no peace of mind, tranquillity, vision of Paradise, Heaven, Angels, the Holy Spirit or God. It is my believe that without the medical attention I was receiving I would have been consumed in the flames, died, and lost for ever, I perceived nothing beyond this world, so must assume there is nothing after death. 'Dust to dust and ashes to ashes.'

The finality of death deprives our successors of the knowledge and experience gained throughout our lives. I therefore believe it is our responsiblity to pass this on through the written and verbal word whilst we are able so to do. The way we live and conduct our lives during the minuscule period of time we have on this planet is all important. The way we respond to, physically help, support and treat our fellow beings is more important and practical than attempting to solve the world's problems on our knees.

We should be thankful for the good things in life when they

exist. Good health, food to eat, employment, a roof over our heads, love and friendship. Yet it would be comforting to know some answers to the unknown: to know there will be another life after death; to know there is a God who looks over and after us; to know the reasons behind so much suffering, selfishness, hatred and greed throughout the world. If there is a God? As yet, he hasn't made himself or answers to these questions known to me.

Billy McCurrie

Student at Baptist College, ex-Loyalist paramilitary

In order to get an idea of who God is and what God is like – in relation to communicable attributes, i.e. wisdom, goodness, righteousness, justice, mercy, love etc. – I need look no further than Jesus.

He loved me before I loved Him, even when I rebelled against His laws and denied His existence He manifested His love and mercy by dying for me on a cross at Calvary and in doing so saved me from eternal death.

He is a friend who remains faithful to me, even when I am unfaithful to Him.

He is to me a father and I am a son to Him, and as a father He disciplines me for my own good when I 'step out of line'.

He brings joy, peace and happiness to troubled hearts and fullness in life to replace the emptiness and superficiality of the world.

God cares for me as an individual and has an interest in me as a person and He is working all things out in my life for my good and His glory. He does not desire my destruction but instruction and seeks to care for me – is it any wonder that I desire to serve and worship Him?

God is just and will punish evil in His own appointed time. Yes, it is true that God is a God of love and mercy, but we must not forget that He is a just God and God's justice demands an eternal death for those who disobey His commands and reject His love, mercy and goodness.

Therefore regarding what happens at death I have no doubt that God turns all those souls into Hell who refuse to gain Heaven through the merits and work of the Lord Jesus Christ, at the cross.

In conclusion, I have no doubt that upon my death I will step from this world into my home in heaven and there – where there will be no more death, sorrow, pain, wars, famine, rebellion, hate, lies, deception, etc. – I will dwell with God in an unbroken relationship forever.

'Anyway, no more having to worry about the central heating bills.'

Jimmy Boyle
Imprisoned for murder, now runs the Gateway Exchange for
ex-convicts

As a kid living in the Gorbals district of Glasgow I was brought
up in a Roman Catholic family. The influence of Catholicism,
therefore, was instilled in me very deeply. I can remember vividly
the first occasion I broke my penance. Having been to Confession to cleanse my soul of its sins in preparation for receiving
Holy Communion at mass the following morning I went into the
streets to play with my pals. During the hotly contested street
games I swore. Like a stroke of lightning I felt a black mark being
chalked across my unstained soul. I felt as though I had violated
something sacred. This carried over to Holy Mass on Sunday
morning. Kneeling on the pews with my family I dreaded the
moment when all of us would be called to receive the holy
sacrament. I agonised at the unfairness of one small swear word
having the power to prevent me from taking part in this particular
part of the ceremony. This incident placed me on the horns of a
dilemma – whose wrath held more sway? As the fateful moment
approached I cocked one eye towards my Mum who, knowing I
had been to confession the previous night, would have ques-
tioned what sins I had committed on seeing me withdraw. My
other eye looked towards the Tabernacle which housed Jesus
Christ. Getting off my knees I preceded my Mum down the aisle
to receive Holy Communion. This first instinctual decision in
challenging Catholicism within myself was the opening of a new
spiritual dimension.

Throughout the darkest years of my earlier life I found myself
many times in the throes of great pain and despair. At such
moments I found myself looking to heaven, searching for a Jesus
Christ to come and sort it out. He didn't. I began to question
some more. Each time I did so I became much stronger as a
person. After many such occasions I came to the realization that

each of us shapes our own life. The more I thought about this the more I came to the conclusion that no superior being or earthly body is going to help me. I now believe, from my own practical experiences, that my God is me. My physical body, which is the vehicle that I travel in through my personal life, will end and that will be it. I will be cremated and thereafter will cease to exist in earthly or heavenly terms.

Roger Daltrey
Musician and actor

God is a spiritual state attained by all knowledge and a complete understanding of everything.

After death my spirit will leave my body, which has served as a 'taxi' for the last life. It will then go through an evaluation of all the knowledge gained. Maybe! No, probably born again for another journey. When my spirit has acquired *all* knowledge then it will become part of the Kingdom of God.

Dr Timothy Leary
LSD guru and author

Everyone gets the God they deserve.
It is a blasphemy against the human spirit to use the word GOD in the singular.
In Gods we trust!

Everyone gets the immortality/death they deserve.

Those who have applied intelligence, good-will, energy to designing and arranging their biological sequence will have many alternatives to passive, involuntary, inevitable metabolic coma.

Sir Fred Hoyle

Astronomer and author

People have raised questions about the meaning of the Universe in all ages, long before there was any chance of answering them in a sensible way. The ancient civilization of Mesopotamia, the Greeks, and our modern society dating from medieval times onward have all built their temples and churches as a continuing expression of man's irrepressible instinct to discover his relation to the Universe at large.

Modern science, as expressed in orthodox biology, denies the validity of this instinct. From the publication in 1859 of Darwin's *The Origins of Species* there has been an insistence that it is all a childish illusion, an insistence drummed in with such persistence that people's ideas have become cloudy and confused. Yet if one summons the courage to shut one's ears to the clamour and take a calm look at the facts, the situation is obviously and manifestly otherwise. Instead of an introverted picture with man crowded in on this particular planet, a prisoner confined to a tiny corner of the solar system, itself but a speck in our galaxy and our galaxy but a speck in the Universe, we have an open picture with life spread throughout the heavens, and quite possibly with life controlling much of what happens everywhere throughout the Universe.

Because of the general harshness of physical conditions, most of life is confined to microorganisms, which can thrive in environments that would be impossible for large multi-celled associations like ourselves. Occasionally, however, where conditions soften, as they did here on the planet Earth, some groups

'Many are called, but few are chosen', ceases to be puzzling if it is interpreted in the present context. Many are the places in the Universe where life exists in its simplest microbial forms, but few support complex multicellular organisms; and of those that do, still fewer have forms that approach the intellectual stature of man; and of those that do, still fewer again avoid the capacity for self-destruction which their intellectual abilities confer on them. Just as the Earth was at a transition point 570 million years ago, so it is today. The spectre of our self-destruction is not remote or visionary. It is ever-present with hands already upon the trigger, every moment of the day. The issue will not go away, and it will not lie around forever, one way or another it will be resolved, almost certainly within a single human lifetime.

If the Earth is to emerge as a place of added consequence, with man of some relevance in the cosmic scheme, we shall need to dispense entirely with the philosophy of opportunism. While it would be no advantage I believe to return to older religious concepts, we shall need to understand why it is that the mysterious sanctity described by Wallace persists within us, beckoning us to the Elysian fields, if only we will follow.

from *The Intelligent Universe*, Michael Joseph, 1983

Bruce Kent

Chair, Campaign for Nuclear Disarmament

Not what, Who. God is Father, Brother, companion and friend. He cares, leads, upholds and gives meaning to hope. He is in mountains, winds and roaring waves but he is also in children's eyes, rabbits and old people walking hand in hand. He is the drive for justice, compassion, generosity and equality. He cares about me. In a crowd he knows my name. I belong to him, whom I see most of all in Jesus the fisherman and carpenter. He is all that is best in life and beauty. But he has left us a mystery which only rarely do we start to understand. He who is all good, tolerates depravity, cruelty and the dreadful sufferings of the innocent. Either this is the price we pay for free will or somehow God is also tied by his creation. Which must be what the Cross is also about.

To be honest I do not think about this very much. I believe in God and trust him totally. But there are questions one cannot answer. No experience of journeys in this life can compare to the passage from the world we know now to the world which, as St Paul says, we now only see as through a glass, darkly. If, as I believe, the wonders of this world and its beauties are only reflections of the glories of God then I am ready to go in confidence.

But how much of 'me' will still be 'me', how that 'me' will relate to those thousands of millions of others, how time that is all at once compares to the time of minutes and hours – all these are mysteries to me. Adults are always asking children what they want to be when they grow up. Children can't really answer. Their 'me' has also to grow. So I feel about death. Let it come when it comes and try to have your bags packed for the journey. But my concern is not with anxieties about the future. It stays with the present in this world where we were told to try to lay the foundations for the Kingdom.

❧ · ❧

That Old Chestnut by Sally Ann Lasson

| SO, I looked up at God | And I said 'God, give me a break' | And he looked down at me and he said | This *is* a break. |

Rev. Dr John Polkinghorne FRS

Professor of Mathematical Physics, Dean and Chaplain of
Trinity Hall, Cambridge

Belief in God means to me that there is a purpose at work in the
world, with a good intent which will not be frustrated, despite all
the bitterness and limitations of life. At the heart of reality there
is One who reigns and loves and forgives. He is also that
Intelligence which is the source of the beautiful order of the
physical world, which science discovers through its inquiry.

What ground is there for such a belief and how is God to be
known? As a Christian I believe that he has acted to reveal
himself in the plainest way possible, by living a human life in
Jesus Christ. The mysterious figure of Jesus, whose words are
pregnant with authority and hope, is one that I have just got to
take into account in framing my understanding of the world. His
life ends in apparent failure, but the Christian insight is that, in
the lonely figure hanging in the darkness and dereliction of the
cross, we see God himself opening his arms to embrace the
bitterness of the world that he has made. The Christian God is
not just a benevolent spectator of the sufferings of humanity, but
he is a fellow-sufferer alongside us.

Something happened between Good Friday and Pentecost to
turn the demoralised disciples into the confident proclaimers of
the Lordship of Christ. I believe that it was the resurrection of
Jesus on Easter Day. If that is true it has two important
consequences. One is that it confirms Jesus as God's chosen one.
The other is that it offers to us, through him, the hope of a
destiny beyond death.

Everyone dies with his or her life in some way incomplete. If
God desires the fulfilment of us all, and if nothing of good is ever
lost in him, then there must be a life beyond this one. When we
die we cannot just be broken pots cast onto the rubbish heap of
the universe. Yet, is it possible in this scientific age to believe in
the hope of a destiny beyond death? I think so. To see how that

could be, one must ask what is the real *me?* It certainly isn't the actual atoms making up my body at some particular instant, since they change all the time, through wear and tear and eating and drinking. I don't think either that the real me is a mysterious spiritual ingredient, trapped within my body, which could be released at death. Instead I think that the real me is the immensely complex information-bearing pattern which at any time is carried by my material body. That pattern is, in fact, the true meaning of the soul. It persists through all the changes of the atoms making me up. At death that pattern is dissolved, but it can be remembered by God and re-created by him in some new environment of his choosing. He is the ultimate, and not death. The hope that I hold is the Christian hope, not of survival, but of death followed by resurrection, through the power of the One who is ever faithful. You could think of it, in a crude sort of way, as being the transfer of software (the pattern that is me) from one set of hardware (my body) to another (the body I will be given in the world to come).

And what will life be like in that future state? Well, we shall have to wait and see. But since I do trust that nothing of good will ever be lost in God, and since human relationships are part of the good of this world, I believe that our relationships with those we love will be restored and healed and fulfilled in that resurrection life. Above all, we shall come to know God with a fullness which will exceed anything we can imagine or even desire. As St Paul said, 'now we see in a mirror dimly, but then face to face'.

Ram Dass (Dr Richard Alpert)

Psychologist and author

What is so enticing is that God is neither a 'who' nor a 'what', nor even a concept. Sometimes in meditation I am able to enter into the space between two thoughts. At that moment the dualism of experiencer and experience disappears, and GOD IS. At other times during devotional practices when the intimacy with the Beloved in any of its myriad forms deepens, there is ultimately a merging with the Beloved and the lover's heart has disappeared. Again, GOD IS.

Through experiences such as these over many years, I find my own identity expanding to embrace the sufferings and joys of others. When I express this compassion arising from unity in action, there are moments, precious indeed, when helper and helped merge into the act itself. Once again, GOD IS.

The words that come to mind about God are 'light', 'beyond yet embracing time and space', 'simplicity', 'unknowable yet be-able', 'form and formless', and, of course, 'love'. And yet the words are not themselves God. Rather they are like fingers pointing at the moon.

Ramana Maharishi, a great Indian saint, said, 'God, Guru, and Self are One'. As I pray more purely and simply, as I honour my Guru more deeply, and as I dive more deeply into my innermost heart, I realize the truth of his words. Only GOD IS.

Walt Whitman wrote, 'To die is different from what anyone supposes and luckier.' I think death is very much like 'taking off a tight shoe,' as a friend once told me. I think it is absolutely safe. The specific experience at the moment of death is very much a function of how much one clings to one's mental constructions of one's identity, and of life and death.

Great mystics who have 'died before they die' are in for no surprises when they leave their body because they had no expectations. They are already identified with pure awareness that is one with God, so the death of their body is merely a flicker of transformation of energy in the ethers, like the disappearance of the light of one tiny star in the galaxy.

Such a spacious scenario is, however, unlikely for most of us who approach death as 'somebody'. For us, a separate conscious-ness, called 'soul' by some, remains. This soul is met by light, by other entities, and sees in a glance its recent incarnation with great clarity and quite devoid of judgement. Immediately after that appreciation, the soul, which is still in time, though of a different dimension than human time, turns towards the future and the subsequent unfolding of karma (or effect).

For those who were least aware in life, there is confusion and dazedness after death. For others there is fear and excitement as images (the ten thousand horrible and the ten thousand beautiful visions) pass before the eye. And for those who are prepared to see the visions as so much dream stuff, there is love and peace.

Arthur C. Clarke

Scientist and author

---

1. I recently told the Papal Nuncio here that I don't believe in God, but I'm very interested in Him.

2. Nothing at all – you just go out like a light!

   For some years I have been worried by the following astrotheological paradox. It is hard to believe that no one else has ever thought of it, yet I have never seen it discussed anywhere.

   One of the most firmly established facts of modern physics, and the basis of Einstein's Theory of Relativity, is that the velocity of light is the speed limit of the material universe. No object, no signal, no *influence*, can travel any faster than this. Please don't ask why this should be; the Universe just happens to be built that way. Or so it seems at the moment.

   But light takes not millions, but *billions*, of years to cross even the part of Creation we can observe with our telescopes. So: if God obeys the laws He apparently established, at any given time He can have control over only an infinitesimal fraction of the Universe. All hell might (literally?) be breaking loose ten light-years away, which is a mere stone's throw in interstellar space, and the bad news would take at least ten years to reach Him. And then it would be another ten years, at least, before He could get there to do anything about it . . .

You may answer that this is terribly naïve – that God is already 'everywhere'. Perhaps so, but that really comes to the same thing as saying that His thoughts, and His influence, can travel at an infinite velocity. And in this case, the Einstein speed limit is not absolute; it *can* be broken.

The implications of this are profound. From the human viewpoint, it is no longer absurd – though it may be presumptuous – to hope that we may one day have knowledge of the most distant parts of the universe. The snail's pace of the velocity of light need not be an eternal limitation, and the remotest galaxies may one day lie within our reach.

But perhaps, on the other hand, God Himself is limited by the same laws that govern the movements of electrons and protons, stars and spaceships. And that may be the cause of all our troubles.

He's coming just as quickly as He can, but there's nothing that even He can do about that maddening 186,000 miles a second.

It's anybody's guess whether He'll be here in time.

from *Report on Planet Three*, Gollancz, 1972

Gerald Priestland
Author and religious affairs correspondent

The day we put God in a box, the World will come to an end.

We shall be given the chance to accept the love of God or to reject it. But even if we accept it, we will still have a long way to go.

The Rt Hon. James Molyneaux JP, MP

Leader of the Official Ulster Unionist Party

As an Anglican layman, I cannot improve on the Nicene Creed.

NICENE CREED

I believe in one God the Father Almighty, Maker of heaven and earth, And of all things visible and invisible:

And in one Lord Jesus Christ, the only-begotten Son of God; Begotten of his Father before all worlds, God of God, Light of Light, Very God of very God; Begotten, not made; Being of one substance with the Father; By whom all things were made: Who for us men and for our salvation came down from heaven, And was incarnate by the Holy Ghost of the Virgin Mary, And was made man: And was crucified also for us under Pontius Pilate; He suffered and was buried: And the third day he rose again according to the Scriptures: And ascended into heaven, And sitteth on the right hand of the Father: And he shall come again, with glory, to judge both the quick and the dead; Whose kingdom shall have no end.

And I believe in the Holy Ghost, The Lord, and Giver of Life, Who proceedeth from the Father and the Son; Who with the Father and the Son together is worshipped and glorified; Who spake by the Prophets: And I believe one Catholic and Apostolic Church: I acknowledge one Baptism for the remission of sins: And I look for the Resurrection of the dead: And the Life of the world to come. Amen.

Book of Common Prayer

Rev. Bernard Green

General Secretary, the Baptist Union of Great Britain
Moderator, Free Church Federal Council 1988–89

◦◦ · ॐ

When I left home as a young man of eighteen during the second
world war to do my national service as a coal-miner the minister
of our church came to a family farewell. He expressed the
pastoral concern of the church and gave me a text from the Bible
to encourage me. It read:

'Be strong and of a good courage. Do not be afraid. For the
Lord your God is with you wherever you go.' (Joshua 1:9)

How wise that minister was! He underlined what my Christian
parents had always taught me, that God is a personal friend and
that real life is built on a trusting relationship with Him. Over the
years I have found that to be profoundly true for myself and for
many people I have known.

God is not a vague Being – 'the One above'. Nor is He a divine
principle, or a code of ethics. He is certainly not a fiction of our
imagination. He is the God made known in the life and ministry
of Jesus Christ. His nature is loving and just, compassionate and
patient. His love has been shown decisively by the forgiving death
of Christ. It is still expressed in the words of the Gospel of St
John – 'God so loved the world that whoever puts trust in Him
shall not perish, but have eternal life'. That makes a personal
relationship with Him crucial to religious faith.

Eternal life, referred to in the previous paragraph, is not to be
thought of simply in terms of life after death. Literally it means
life of the new age, life in a new dimension. The nitty-gritty of
daily existence in the world as it really is still has to be faced. But
life can have the quality of God's love, truth, peace and goodness
at its heart through faith in Jesus Christ. This sets everything in a
new perspective.

That is a life which death cannot destroy. My old minister used
to remind us in his preaching that Jesus said, 'I am the
resurrection and the life; whoever trusts in me, though he dies,

yet shall he live.' And he would go on – 'Therefore whoever has Jesus has the resurrection!' I believe that. I cannot prove it; but it is true to the teaching of the Bible and it is basic to my Christian faith that past, present and future, whatever happens, are firmly in the care of a God we can trust. So I do not try to speculate about life after death. To be in the love of God is enough. Despite all my natural questions and doubts I trust Him.

Pir Vilayat Inayat Khan
Head of the Sufi Order of the West

My father Hazrat Inayat Khan once said what we usually think is God is actually our concept of God. Therefore the question you ask me puts me in the position of formulating yet one more concept in your collection while eschewing the reality behind it all. However, my father did realize the value of a concept as a stepping stone to the real thing, which is the experience of God. Actually we need to be wary of that word 'experience', because it illustrates the most primary mode of cognizance where the existential realm is looked upon as the object cognized by a subject – the inevitable subject-object dichotomy, whereas in our higher modes of cognizance we realize that our thinking is the thinking of the universe and, as St Francis of Assisi said, 'that which is experienced is that which experiences'. This is why for the Sufis, God can never be the object of our experience, but is the Experiencer and our consciousnesses are like branches of that experiencer. Therefore He/She cannot be known as an object other than ourselves, but as the ground of our consciousness. Moreover He/She does become in us the object of His/Her Self-discovery inasmuch as our personality manifests and even existentiates His/Her Nature.

Matter never dies, it undergoes changes, gradual ones (as radiation, osmosis, ageing) and also sudden ones, like in a quantum leap (water into steam, the jump of an electron from one orbital of the atom to another, what we call death).

In the evolutionary leap from the inorganic to the organic, the electrons within the atom rearrange themselves more meaningfully and efficiently as a support system for the advance of intelligence and consciousness than in the previous arrangement. Hastily observed, the devastating eclipse in the in-between stage could easily be misconstrued as a falling apart. Never does the same water flow under the same bridge, yet the river remains. Judged from the point of view of the particular drops, it looks as though they have eluded one's gaze. If a magnetic field structuring metal filings into a pattern were to undergo a momentary depolarization and then get polarized, perhaps with a different voltage, the metal filings would disperse, then reform again no doubt differently. The reality of the frequency pattern of the magnet is more importantly attributable to the magnet; the outer pattern of the metal filings is secondary. The reality of our body is not the visible structure, but what Dr Rupert Sheldrake calls the 'morphic resonance' which is more basic than the building blocks and survives their demise, while mutating over the aeons of time. If you take a computer apart, just examining the chips, it would be difficult to figure out the software, but if you know the software, you are in possession of the key that would enable you to make computers. If after death you have freed yourself from the support system, you don't need the hardware anymore. After the quantum leap we call death, then the protons and electrons of the body get scattered in the universe. Owing to the limitation of the speed of light, they cannot communicate by the kind of signalling that we encounter in the universe in its explicate state, but they are still interconnected, say the physicists, in a 'non-local' state, the implicate state, while confounding our minds by not conforming to our ideas about causality. Each sub-atomic particle stores some information (in its spin) and the particles form together the network that acts as a support system for our minds, and consciousnesses. If you have experienced even a flash of out-of-body travel, you will realize that indeed one can continue to see without eyes, hear without ears, displace oneself without wings, communicate without language signals and understand without involving the brain.

While one may grasp splendour as it transpires through a

scene of beauty, one can moreover grasp splendour directly irrespective of or bereft of its physical support system. And while one's understanding is usually based upon the assessment of a situation, one may moreover grasp meaningfulness directly – a kind of feed-forward instead of a feed-back.

Information is built up at the cost of the expenditure of its support system: energy (negenthropy); this is precisely what is meant by resurrection. Besides we need to distinguish between the knowledge that we attain by processing and interpreting the input from outside i.e. (reacting to circumstances and adapting ourselves with conditions), and a kind of pre-cognizance irrespective of the feedback of experience. In philosophy it is called proto-critic knowledge. Imagine the mind, having built its constructs on experiencing other than itself, now discovering meaningfulness within itself, because our minds are isomorphic, homologous with (that is, of the same nature as) the mind of the universe and co-extensive with that global mind we call the mind of God. Even as the global mind, so our mind which actuates that mind is self-generating. A good example in Greek mythology is Belaphron abandoning his steed Pegasus (the support system of the mind) who could reach no further and proceeding on his own to the Olympus! 'The tendency of the soul is to reach to the highest spheres to which it belongs, but it cannot rise from the lower regions until it has left behind all earthly attachments', said Hazrzrat Inayat Khan. Do you ever feel that your body cannot contain you or constrain you or live up to the thrust of your mind or withstand the exhilaration of your soul? These are the vistas attained in the farther reaches of the mind where illumination flashes as realization. Here meditation will help one have a foretaste of life after death.

Imagine that you have awakened from your commonplace perspective, having shaken off that perspective like a snake of its skin, and remember having been caught in that bind (in the mind). For one who values splendour the software of the universe is more thrilling than the hardware. I have a hunch that after death, if one has awakened, while still getting flashes of the manifestation of the divine intention transpiring from a distant perspective, one highlights that intention grasped directly so that its manifestation is secondary and in the twilight of consciousness. One may prepare oneself for this in meditation with open eyes by, as the Sufis say, always looking for the hallmark of the divine intention behind all occurrence.

According to some testimonies at the eleventh hour, at the moment of death, one's life on the Planet comes to a head: that which was accomplished, that which one failed at, one's assets and one's defects or foibles, the harm one did to others, one's resentment for those who offended one, the ruthless and inexorable unexpected we call fate, one's loves and enmities, hopes and disappointments, struggles and satisfactions, all interweave into an evanescent kaleidoscopic pattern upon the screen of the mind.

By dint of the interfacing and interreacting of the plethora of elements flashing over the threshold between the unconscious and the conscious, the issues enacted in one's life pattern and the challenge matched or mis-matched by our resourcefulness, or what we made of our resourcefulness suddenly zooms into perspective. Dr Kubler Ross once pointed out that one is assailed with the remorse of not having done those things one could have done, but more desperately, for not having become what one might have become. I like to add 'how one could have been if one would have been what one might have been'. Here lie the crucial issues – particularly the latter. Obviously it would have been wiser to have dealt with this earlier; or rather let us deal with the paramount issue now: our personality.

Three parameters strike one: (i) unfurling the resourcefulness lying dormant in our heritage from the whole universe as much in its enormous compass as at all its levels; (ii) customizing these creatively according to our own bent or peculiar genius by rearranging these, fluctuating these like variations on a theme, and confronting and sharpening these by the encounter with the challenge of our lives; (iii) transmuting these so as to extract the essence of these like the perfume out of flowers.

In the early stages of one's life the first seems to prevail; in the middle of life's struggle, the second; at the autumn of one's life, the third: one needs to learn to resurrect before death. This requires pruning, assessing priorities, freeing oneself from a lot of ballast, most importantly identifying oneself with the perfume extracted from that flower that was our personality with its many idiosyncrasies; that is, its petals which will need to fall apart so that the perfume may prevail.

Hasan abdu'l-Hakim

The Islamic Cultural Centre, London

—— ◦ ◦ ——

The first part of the Muslim confession of faith (the *shahada*) is the basis for the concept of God in Islam. The Muslim bears witness that: 'There is no god but God', or 'no divinity but the (one) Divinity'. The revealed Scripture of Islam, the Qur'an, is like a vast commentary on this simple statement, drawing from it all its implications for human life and thought.

This conception of the Deity is strictly monotheistic and unitarian. God alone has absolute *being*, totally independent and totally self-sufficient. Whatever exists or ever could exist does so by His will. He has no 'partner' either in creating the universe or in maintaining it in existence. He is not only the 'First Cause' but also ultimately, the only cause, and He is Himself uncaused. The Qur'an tells us: 'Say: He is Allah, One, the utterly Self-sufficient: He begets not neither is He begotten, and there is nothing that is like unto Him.' It tells us also that: 'When He wills a thing to be, He but says unto it, "Be!" and it *is*.'

In the Islamic view, it is impossible for the human mind to form an adequate conception of God as He is in His eternal and absolute being. The creature cannot comprehend the Creator. According to the Qur'an, 'No (human) vision encompasseth Him, yet He encompasseth (all) vision.'

He is *al-Ahad*, 'the One', absolute unity. This is in sharp contrast to the Christian conception of the Trinity. The One cannot be divided, nor can it be diminished or 'humanised' by incarnation in any created form. God does not become His own creature, in fact He does not 'become' anything: He *is*.

He is *al-Awwal*, 'the First' before whom there is nothing, and *al-Akhir*, 'the Last', after whom there is nothing; but He is not only at the beginning and at the end of time, for He is also *al-Zahir*, 'the Outward', present behind all the shifting scenes we perceive in the world around us, and *al-Batin*, 'the Inward', for it is His power that moves and motivates all that exists.

He is not only *al-Khāliq*, 'the Creator', who gives each separate thing the light of existence by His command, 'Be!', but He is also *al-Musawwir* who 'shapes' it in accordance with the nature He wishes it to have, for everything in the world has its purpose and is moulded to serve that purpose.

When creatures have been brought into existence and fashioned in accordance with the divine purpose, they are not abandoned and left to fend for themselves. Two very particular 'names' stand at the very centre of the Islamic concept of God. These are *al-Rahmān* and *al-Rahīm*. Both are derived from the Arabic word for 'Mercy', *Rahma*, which is closely related to the word for 'womb' and therefore carries with it implications of creativeness and fecundity. In one of the inspired sayings in which God spoke to mankind through the Prophet Muhammad we are told that His 'Mercy' takes precedence over His 'Wrath'.

Despite this outpouring of mercy, we still go astray, for man – as the Qur'an tells us – was 'created weak', and our situation might seem hopeless if God were not *al-Tawwāb*, 'the Relenting', who never tires of turning back to His creatures when they turn to him in repentance. He is *al-Ghaffār*, 'the Ever-Forgiving', and *al-'Afū*, 'the Effacer (of sins)'. Whatever people may do in the course of their lives they have the opportunity to seek his forgiveness so long as they have breath, but the opportunity is lost when death comes and, after that, they are judged for what they are or for what they have made of themselves. So the Qur'an says: 'O My servants who have damaged your own selves, despair not of the Mercy of Allah. Truly Allah pardons all sins. Truly He is the Forgiving, the Merciful. So turn unto your Lord repentant and surrender unto Him before the punishment comes upon you; then ye will not be helped.'

But 'sinning' and 'going astray' would have no clear meaning if God had not shown His creatures the right way, the 'straight path' as it is called in the Qur'an. One of His names is *al-Hādi*, 'the Guide'. We are assured that He has never left any nation or any group of people without guidance; to each He has sent a 'messenger' to deliver them a 'message' of hope and guidance and to instruct them as to how to follow the 'straight way' which leads to Paradise and, ultimately, to *al-Ridwān*, the 'Good Pleasure' or 'Satisfaction' of God Himself. These divine 'messages' have been clothed in the language and thought-patterns of the people to whom they were addressed so as to be clear and unambiguous, and the 'messengers' who have been the instruments of this guidance have been men like other men, though in every way better than others.

In spite of their clarity, these 'messages' have again and again been rejected by many of those to whom they were addressed, and it is precisely this freedom to reject the truth that distinguishes man from the other creatures who share the earth with us – the animals, the birds and the fishes. They follow by instinct the way set before them, the law of their species, but mankind has the unique freedom either to follow the 'straight path' consciously and deliberately or to turn away from it and follow the dictates of self-will. Man alone has been given a mind capable of understanding the truth, a will capable of choosing the path of truth, and a heart inclined by its very nature to love the truth.

'For each of you have We appointed a divine Law and a way of life,' says the Qur'an. 'Had Allah so willed, He could have made you one people; but, so that He may try you by that which He hath bestowed upon you (He hath willed otherwise). So compete in doing good. Unto Allah ye will all return, and He will inform you regarding that wherein ye differ.' In terms of this and other similar verses, it is entirely possible for Muslims to accept the idea that the pre-Islamic religions were at least partial statements of the One Truth, adapted to time and place and to the spiritual needs of different peoples.

The Muslim, however, believes that the message brought by the Prophet Muhammad completes the vast structure of revelation and provides a final synthesis, after which there is nothing more to be said. Judaism and Christianity are both 'monotheistic' religions, but Muslims consider that the Jews falsely appropriated the universal Truth, claiming it as the property of one single people, while the Christians distorted it through the doctrines of the Trinity and the Incarnation. In the Islamic view, the 'message' transmitted through Muhammad represented, not a completely new religion, but a corrective to the falsifications and distortions which had taken place and, at the same time, an uncompromising re-assertion of the pure doctrine of the One God.

Islam asserts that the present life is but a minute part of the totality of existence. The Qur'an informs man of the reality of another Life of a very different nature from the life of this world, of infinite duration. For God, the All-Wise, All-Powerful Creator, is able to do anything He pleases, and He is easily able to transform His creations from one state of being to another. Can we for a moment imagine that it can be more difficult for Almighty God to raise us up when we are dead than it was to create us in the first place? The Qur'an speaks again and again of familiar and obvious examples of such transformations: the coming to life again of the earth after it lies dead and barren in the grip of winter or drought; the development of a sperm and an ovum into an embryo in the environment of the mother's womb, and its further development from that state into a thinking, feeling, acting human being living in the world.

> And among His signs is this: Thou seest the earth barren and desolate, but when We send down rain to it, it is stirred to life and yields increase. Verily, He Who gives life to the (dead) earth can surely give life to the dead. Lo! He has power over all things. (41:39)

Islam lays the greatest stress on the individual's accountability to God. The human being's life in this world constitutes a trial, an examination period, during which he prepares himself, either for good or for ill, for the next Life of infinite duration. The Day of Judgement may be compared to the ending of the examination, during which the Teacher will ask each individual student, 'What were you doing during the exam?' and will then evaluate the work he hands in. For although man's body dies, his soul, his personality has an existence extending beyond the present life; it is a continuous entity whose inner state will accompany it into the Hereafter. It is this state, together with one's deeds, which will determine one's ultimate destiny.

It is obvious that an individual who has lived with the correct awareness of and relationship to Reality through submission to God Most High is in an entirely different inner state from one who has lived all his life with an incorrect or distorted awareness of Reality and in forgetfulness, rebellion and ingratitude vis-à-vis God, and who has died in this state. Moreover, although many of the deeds of such people may appear outwardly similar, they have been motivated by entirely different intentions: the one to obey and please God and the other for any reason other than pleasing God, Whose reality he does not acknowledge. Indeed, the differences between the inner states of such persons is so great that their being kept apart from one another, in entirely different environments corresponding to what is within them and among companions having a similar inner condition, is a requirement of the most rudimentary conception of justice, not to speak of the absolute, unswerving justice of the All-Knowing, All-Wise, Infinitely Just and at the same time Most Merciful God.

In very vivid, awe-inspiring language, the Qur'an sketches over and over the outline of the events of the Last Day. At a time when God sees fit, which is known only to Him, this world will be brought to an end in a terrifying cosmic cataclysm frightful beyond imagination. And on that awesome Day of Judgement, the bodies of the dead will be raised from their graves and rejoined with their souls, while those who were alive on earth at that time will die and be joined to this assembly. All men, past and present, will then stand before God, each one as totally alone and helpless as when he came into the world, to render their accounting.

Then those who denied God and rejected His guidance, who devoted themselves to the worship of deities other than God, and who did evil deeds will be consigned to a fearsome and terrible abode in which their companions will be others who, like themselves, are completely alienated from God. There they will be in a state of enduring torment and agony from which there will be no respite. They will long to have another chance to return to the world to live their lives differently in the light of their present knowledge of Reality but it will be too late; the examination will be over and all the books closed, and they will have no choice but to acknowledge the justice of their destiny which is due to what their own hands wrought, in spite of all the clear warnings which were sent to guide them.

> Verily, the sinners will be in the punishment of Hell, to remain therein. It will not be lightened for them and they will be overwhelmed in despair. And We shall not be unjust to them, but it is they who have been unjust to themselves. (43:74–76)

As for those who believed in God, who obeyed and submitted to Him and lived their lives for His pleasure, and who left this life in a state of surrender to Him, a state of unutterable contentment and satisfaction awaits:

> Those who believe and do righteous deeds, they are the best of creatures. Their reward is with their Lord: Gardens of Paradise beneath which rivers flow. They will dwell therein forever, God well-pleased with them and they with Him. This is for those who hold their Lord in awe. (98: 7–8)

These two states, Heaven and Hell, will be experienced in physical form by the new bodies with which God will raise men up; they are not merely spiritual or psychic states. And while we do not know their exact nature, the Qur'an tells us that the inhabitants of Heaven will experience some things which will remind them of their life on earth, that the happiness and beauty of it will far exceed anything one can imagine, and that the ultimate triumph and bliss for those who have attained Paradise will be in nearness to their Lord. As for those who have deserved Hell, theirs will be a temporary or permanent state of torture depending on their inner condition and the nature and extent of their sins. The Qur'an describes Hell as a state of intense, fearful burning and agony without respite, among the most horrifyingly loathsome surroundings and companions. But the most awful part of the suffering of its inhabitants will be the terrible, inescapable awareness that this is the destiny which they deserved and brought upon themselves by rejecting God and ignoring the guidance which He had conveyed to them through His messengers.

This clear reality of the future Life is always before the mind and consciousness of the devout Muslim. It is this awareness which keeps the present life, in the midst of the most intense happiness and the deepest pain alike, in perspective: the perspective of a passing, temporary abode in which one has been placed as a test in order to qualify and prepare himself for his future Home. This perspective is essential for the maintenance of mental balance and stability amidst the difficulties of life. Yet no Muslim, even the best among them, imagines that he is guaranteed Paradise; on the contrary, the more conscientious and God-fearing one is, the more he is aware of his own shortcomings and weaknesses. Therefore the Muslim, knowing that God alone controls life and death, and that death may come to him at any time, tries to send on ahead for his future existence such deeds as will merit the pleasure of his Lord, so that he can look forward to it with hope for His mercy and grace.

from *Islam and Muslims* by Suzanne Haneef,
Kazi Publications, 1979.

James Sturzaker
Principal, International Order Of Kabbalists

․

I believe in a supreme Creative Force that is pure mind/energy. There is nothing in manifestation or in the unmanifest that IT did not create out of Itself. I use the term 'IT' because I believe the creative Force has both masculine and feminine principles containing positive and negative potencies in equal potential. Therefore, in Itself it is perfect balance and unity. It is only at the different levels of manifestation that imbalance and disharmony occur due to humanity having received a degree of free will.

The 'Gods' of the various religions are, to me, the lesser Gods or aspects of the one supreme Creative Force, just as the archangels, angels and other manifestations of the supreme consciousness, including humanity, are also aspects at a lower level of this same Creative Force. To me, the human kingdom is spirit clothed in matter.

First, I must say that I do not believe that anyone dies in the generally accepted sense. There is only Life in various states of consciousness whether we are wearing a physical overcoat of form or are formless. When we depart from the physical world we proceed to another dimension and undergo experiences there as we have done in this physical universe. This procedure is continued throughout the many dimensions of existence until eventually we have reached a perfected state of being on each plane of consciousness and are enabled to return to the source from which we emanated, our true home.

Since it is highly unlikely that any one of us could attain to perfection in one short physical lifetime this brings me to reincarnation. It is my firm belief that we return to the physical universe as many times as it takes to undergo all the experiences necessary for our development and spiritual progress. This occurs on the other planes of consciousness also until we are fit to be absorbed back into the Oneness that ever is.

Rev. Oral Roberts
Christian Evangelist

Who is God? What is He like? First, God is Spirit. The Bible teaches,

> God is a spirit and they that worship Him, must worship Him in spirit and truth.
>
> John 4:24

Second, His rank is supreme. His power and reign transcend all earthly kingdoms and all human thrones and powers. He is the supreme Source of all power . . . all knowledge . . . all wisdom.

God is the only self-existing being, not dependent upon anything or anybody. He fills the heavens and the earth, governing and upholding all things. In Him, we live and move and have our being.

Third, He is the cause of all good things, the fountain of all perfection. He is the Source of all that is love . . . all that is pure . . . all that is true . . . all that provides benefit. He created all of life and made man His masterpiece.

God's very nature is good. His spirit is perfect love. He longs to supply the needs of His people. He longs to communicate with each one of us. And He comes to us in different ways. One person may need a loud, large, or overwhelming experience. God will come to that person that way. Another may need a quiet conviction and reassurance of His presence. The Lord will come to him in that manner.

Fourth, God is eternal. He has always been, He is now and He will be forever. Nothing precedes Him, nothing outlasts Him.

Because God is Spirit and a spirit cannot be seen or understood easily, God sent His Son, Jesus Christ of Nazareth, in the likeness of flesh to reveal God to us. And what was Jesus like? He was perfect in power. The raging storms . . . all manner of sickness and disease . . . even death itself gave to His healing, delivering power. He held supreme rank over all spiritual beings; demons fled from His presence. He gave good to everyone He encountered in whom He found faith and a desire for God's presence. He healed the broken, maimed, sick, and troubled. He provided for every need. And He, too, is eternal. He's alive today, having risen from the grave and ascended into heaven, where He is seated at the right hand of God forever to be our advocate, counsellor, and Saviour. He is my Lord.

To the believer and follower of Christ Jesus, death is instant transference into the Lord's presence. Instant! The moment death takes the body, at that very instant we're absent from the physical body and at home with the Lord (2 Corinthians 5:8). And the Bible says, 'We shall be made like Him.' That means it is the time of our final and complete *healing*. Everything that prayer missed or the doctors missed, the Resurrection of Jesus is going to get. We'll have no more disease, weakness or affliction. We'll be free from tormenting worry, temptation and all the results of sin. We'll experience His perfection in a full and complete way. The Scriptures say, 'Blessed are the dead which died in the Lord', (Revelation 14:13). That means, as believers in Christ Jesus, whether we live or die, we are *in* the Lord. Death has no sting for us (1 Corinthians 15:53–57). It is only our transition to a new and glorious existence in His presence – the hope of every grieving person, the desire of every Christian. To a Christian, our death day is better than our birthday! For the rewards of that *eternal* life are beyond even our best and brightest imaginations.

Kingsley Amis CBE
Novelist

᳇ᦢ · ᦣᦢ

Here are the answers to your two questions.

None

Nothing

Even though you suggest that you will be printing replies from such horrible people as the Archbishop of Canterbury, Peter Ustinov and Spike Milligan, I hereby give you permission to quote my answers to your questions.

Walter Schwarz
Religious Affairs Correspondent, the *Guardian*

᳇ᦢ · ᦣᦢ

I would call God an intuitively sensed order and meaning in life which goes beyond the scientifically provable and includes beauty and love. I do not conceive of this God as a person, only as a force, or a dimension of reality. But beauty and love imply morality and morality implies an inner dialogue between sinner and judge. In that sense, God is not entirely impersonal either.

I do not believe anything happens to me when I die, other than death, because I am inseparable from life. I consider it possible that a spiritual dimension of my being might have come from God, as defined above, and might in some sense rejoin God after

my death and even inhabit a new body. But this is an abstract concept for me, not especially comforting, still less a motivating faith. In any conceivable world, virtue has to be its own reward.

The Rt Hon. Viscount Tonypandy
PC, DCL
◆ · ◆

Firstly my concept of God is not of a human being. I believe that the human mind is incapable of understanding anything other than that God is like Jesus. We know the nature of God because it has been revealed to us through Christ our Lord. Because my concept of Him is of a Father it leads me naturally to regard all men as brothers.

In my judgement therefore the brotherhood of man is the natural consequence of accepting the Fatherhood of God.

Secondly I believe that there is a life beyond death. I do not look for a physical resurrection but that there is a spiritual eternity for each of us is my firm belief, because I put my trust in the resurrection of Jesus Christ.

Rev. The Lord Soper
Former President, Methodist Conference

◆ · ◆

I remember an occasion many years ago, in the open air on Tower Hill, I was speaking about God and a friendly heckler suggested that I really had no idea as to what, or who, God was like. Moreover he claimed that all spiritual concepts were quite arbitrary. As if to prove his point he asked me what shape was the soul. I told him 'oblong' and I'm afraid that in the ensuing merriment the argument was not pursued much further. If it had been on that day, or indeed if it is to be seriously considered, I am sure that the concept of God is, in thinking terms, the all important issue for us human beings. Further I am equally sure that however diligent or wise we may become we shall never in this lifetime come to a final and complete answer. Yet I believe there is a sufficient answer for us pilgrims on this planet. I have found that Jesus is the 'human photograph' of God – which is another way of saying that Jesus is the Way, the Truth and the Life of God. Such is the life of Jesus presented to God's children in the only concept and language they can understand, and can use as a means of communication and franchise. But it is enough for the time being.

If the foregoing is true, as I believe, then we are encouraged to look to Jesus for help in making up our minds as to what happens when we die. I confess that I am taking a more proximate interest in this matter as I contemplate my increasing age. I further confess that I find the precise pronouncements about the next world, if any, most unsatisfactory. The prospect of an existence beyond time and space as well as beyond matter is incomprehensible. I haven't the mental equipment with which to deal with it.

Yet I am not comfortless in as much as Jesus makes no attempt to provide that specific information. He neither included it in his teaching ministry nor offered it to his disciples when he came back to them from the other side of death. What he did say was that in the Father's House were many mansions, that he was going on ahead to prepare them for his followers, and that should be sufficient comfort and assurance of an infinitely worthwhile future beyond the grave. That gospel will do for me, while I remain principally concerned not with what will happen when I die but how to live now so as to inherit the promise of Jesus in the eternal love of God.

━━━━━━━━━━━━━━━━━━━ ⋯ · ⋯ ━━━━━━━━━━━━━━━━━━━

Death is for many of us the gate of hell; but we are inside on the way out, not outside on the way in.   – George Bernard Shaw

Anglican Archbishop of Armagh, Primate of All Ireland

The Most Rev. Dr R. H. A. Eames

Personally I find myself wondering when I think of a deep theological approach to the meaning of God and compare that to my own experience of God at work in people's lives. On the one hand I accept how God has been revealed to people through the ages: by the life and teaching of Jesus, by the Traditions of the Church, by the words of the Bible and by the doctrines of the Church. On the other hand there is the deeply personal nature of God as a Father to mankind, making Himself real and alive through His love and influence in our lives as ordinary people. It is in this latter sense that most people who claim to be Christians look for His Presence and most expect to find Him each day they live.

To put it plainly: there is the God as expressed in theological or doctrinal language and there is the God of personal experience and personal knowledge.

God is a very personal dimension in my own life. I believe that the evidence of His existence must be felt rather than proved. I believe He chose to show us His real nature through the life of His Son, Jesus Christ, and I believe that my response to Him must begin by this recognition but move on to a life dedicated to serve Him, worship Him and help others to find His love in their own lives. I cannot imagine how I could cope with ordinary life without that belief. Of course I have my moments of doubt and uncertainty – and I have questions I cannot answer easily about the nature and presence of a God of love. But in the end I see so much evidence of the power of His love at work in the world in the lives of people I meet and work with, that I know in my own heart and mind He must be at the centre of what I call human experience.

It always fascinates me when a little child at school attempts to draw a picture of God. We see drawings of a great figure controlling the world or a bearded figure in eastern dress. We see drawings of someone they love such as a parent or we see attempts at very traditional Biblical scenes. How rarely we see a drawing of a figure of fear or terror.

In the violence of Northern Ireland I have seen so many examples of how God's strength and God's presence in the lives of ordinary people has brought comfort, reconciliation and a deep desire to rise above suffering or bereavement.

I find there can be only one explanation for the evidence of my own eyes: there exists a God of genuine love and compassion and people want to respond to Him.

So my personal concept of God is that of a Father who creates, cares and loves people as they are and gives them an opportunity to become something better than they are through the example of His Son, Jesus Christ.

If I am to be completely honest I find much more peace of mind and satisfaction in this personal experience of God's love than I do when I try to come to grips with the niceties of Church teaching and doctrine about the nature of God. The teaching of the Church gives me an intellectual satisfaction – the personal daily walk in which I try to find His will for me as a person is the reality which gives me the greatest sense of purpose for living.

This is a question which has confronted people since the beginning of time. The real mystery comes from the fact that we are thinking of the unknown. So many aspects of life are known to us all because we have seen them, felt them or experienced them – people have told us about them or we have passed through them ourselves. When we talk about death we know what it is like to see others die, to feel what it is like to miss people we love when they die or to see the effect on someone when they know they are going to die.

But for most of us the actual action of dying is something that happens to other people. We find it very hard to place ourselves as a person in that position.

So much of what people think about death stems from a fear of the unknown. Fear is one of the most devastating emotions we can experience. It results from many factors in life, but in the end it means the same thing. We feel we cannot face up to something or someone because of what might happen to us.

If I see God as a God of love and compassion I cannot believe that the love I feel in this life can be ended by the physical experience of death. If I believe in His care for me as a person then I cannot accept that that relationship will end when I die. If I accept what Christ said and taught and particularly if I believe in the Resurrection of Christ after Calvary, then I cannot doubt that life in some form continues after death.

I cannot accept that the beauty and sense of purpose of life I find in knowing and loving God in this world can end without meaning or purpose at the grave. The experience of God that is such a powerful force in my life now points me continually towards the hope and certainty of even greater love and knowledge when I die. I cannot describe what that new life will be like or what form it will take, but I am convinced the existence of life beyond the grave in the nearer presence of a God of love is the only way to make sense out of a great deal that happens in this present life.

In the end it is because I believe in a God of love that all fear of death disappears. In its place is the fascination of what it will be like and what more it will show me of a God whose whole Being speaks to me of love.

The Anglican Archbishop of Cape Town
The Most Rev. Desmond M. Tutu DD, FKC

Definitely WHO. God is our Father both as Creator and in His continuing and amazing love for each individual irrespective of her/his response to that love. I conceive of Him as Father as that is the best I can do in human terms to describe the indescribable, for He is so much more. Since to be human is to be created in His image each person is of infinite worth, a God-carrier through whom we may experience the divine.

Nothing, or at least nothing more than a passing quietly from a room where you have been talking with your family and friends into another where they can no longer see you. But the house is God's. He created it, He is there and may be encountered at any time. To be with Him is unspeakable joy. Death gives us the opportunity to realize our full potential and become what He created us to be, perfect, even as He is perfect in order that we may fulfil our unique role in the great harmony of creation.

Father Andrew Byrne

Priest of Opus Dei

What do I think about God and life after death? A welcome question. God is everything to me, so the very question 'What do you think about God?' makes me glad. I remember an Everley Brothers' song which said: 'All I need to do is dream'.

But with God it isn't just a dream. He's real. Yes, God, you're real, more real than the things I'm most convinced about, my eyes, my hands . . .

God is everything, for me

What do I think of you, God? I would run round the world a thousand times to find you, that's how I feel. I could be talking to you and about you all day and all night long.

You are the one who gives me my breath; this very moment, if my heart is beating, it is you that makes it beat. God, you are my Father; you are Jesus, my Brother; you are, most Holy Spirit, my love and lover. I feel just a teeny twinge of envy (not really!) of women here. The difference of the sexes and the fact that we address you, my God, as He, means that women can more promptly understand that you want to be loved by us. But we men too are called to love you with all the fire of our heart, fearlessly, because God will purify our love. There is no danger of loving you too passionately.

You are such a wonderful lover that you tell us 'With me, it's all or nothing'. Some misunderstand this and speak of you (they don't know you) as tyrannical. How wrong they are! When lovers really love, they want the best for their lover. But human beings tend to run out of steam. You, my God, don't. So you ask all. You pay us the compliment of appreciating everything we have.

I see you in a woman (or man) growing old. How I would like to shout to her or him, 'You're not growing old and useless!' A swimmer at 20, a footballer at 30, ready for the scrap heap? Not at all! My God you are still in her, in him: if they let you in there's so much they can do!

I look forward to being with Him for ever in heaven

I firmly believe that the real life is life after death, with God.

However, I'd better begin with what will happen as soon as I die.

First, I hope many will pray for me, because once I die I will be judged. Every thought, word and deed of mine will be judged, unappealably. Frightening! But I will have my Guardian Angel and Mary, the Blessed Virgin, speaking up for me. The judge will be Jesus. The better I have loved Him on earth, the less afraid I will be.

I won't speak of hell, except to say I firmly believe it exists and that it's not difficult to get there; but I pray with all my heart that, through the merits of Christ, its population will end up as close to nil as possible (it's the one place where I would like to see a restrictive population policy!). But, it would be most foolish to forget that only those who love God will be saved.

Then, purgatory, for those who still carry some stains of sin. Purgatory is 'hell-with-a-purpose', a place of excruciating pain (worse than any earthly pain; so, whenever we think, 'This is hell', because of a splitting headache, let's stop and say, 'No, it isn't. And I'll offer it up for the souls in purgatory').

And Heaven. What will it be like? 'Neither eye has seen, no ear heard, nor human heart conceived, the welcome God has prepared for those who love him' (1 Corinthians 2:9). Every fibre in our body, every aspiration of our soul, will find true, living, thrilling happiness in lovingly looking at, enjoying, possessing God, my God, my Love, for ever. And our loved ones too.

Joyful memories can help us imagine. Ginger Rogers and Fred

Astaire 'in heaven . . . when we're out together dancing cheek to cheek'; Mitzi Gaynor singing in *South Pacific* 'I'm in love with a wonderful guy'. Swimming, dancing, flying, all free, and pure, sheer joy, uncontaminated, an ecologist's paradise! I remember at the age of twelve swimming in midsummer in the Lake of Geneva, near Montreux. The water was deliciously warm, perfectly calm; one could plunge into the depths, and feel enveloped: looking upon the Blessed Trinity will be that, plunging into the immeasurable depths of God, and much, much more.

Finally, the important thing is not to talk about God but to love Him, not to talk about Heaven but to get there. To help us, Jesus has given us a special gentle hand, that of His (and our) Mother Mary.

Rabbi Dr Sidney Brichto

Executive Vice-President and Director, The Union of Liberal
and Progressive Synagogues

❦ · ❦

'Where is the dwelling of God?'
This was the question with which the rabbi of Kotzk surprised
a number of learned men who happened to be visiting him.
They laughed at him: 'What a thing to ask! Is not the whole
world full of his glory!'
Then he answered his own question:
'God dwells wherever man lets him in.'

from *Tales of the Hasidim*

Like most Jewish children, I believed that God looked very much
like Michelangelo's Moses. He was demanding as well as All-
Mighty and I had to be good to avoid incurring his anger. What
he would do to me for being bad, I never figured out. Probably, I
did not want to think too deeply on it, just as one does not like to
think what would happen were there to be a nuclear war.

When I read more of the Bible and Jewish literature, God
developed a more complicated personality. He was more loving
and emotional. He had a heart and he did not always have it his
own way. The story of Abraham bargaining over the fate of the
inhabitants of Sodom and Gomorrah left a deep impression upon
me. It is an unusual God who feels obligated to tell Abraham that
he is going to destroy the wicked twin cities and is willing to
accept his criticism: 'Will you sweep away the innocent along
with the guilty? Will not the Judge of all the earth act justly?' God
agrees to spare the cities if there are fifty righteous men and is
then wheedled to spare them if there are only ten. Abraham
demands justice and mercy from God and he gets his way.

This right of man to make demands upon God and to express
dissatisfaction with the Creator of the Universe became an
important part of my faith. It enabled me to hold on to my
conviction of the existence of God even after the world seemed

like a godless place once the horrors of the Nazi terror became known. I conceive of God as the creator and inspiration of all that is good and rational in the world. He is not an omnipotent God, but a God who, like an artist, has to work with the material at His disposal. These are the non-rational forces which have to be conquered and controlled. Men and women were created to help Him achieve this. They must use the creativity with which God has endowed them to control nature and to predict its course so as to limit its potential for catastrophe. Of course, all this is pointless unless they learn to subdue the irrational evil and blindness within themselves which leads to far greater human destruction than any natural disaster. This can best be done by the conviction that there is a Power for good in the universe whom we call God, who can inspire in man the faith that all is achievable, even his own moral perfection. Can anyone doubt that were we to make the same progress in moral behaviour that we have made in the arts and sciences, the world would not be a safer and more beautiful place?

Many will feel that my concept of a limited God is not the God in whom they have been taught to believe, but *this* is the God I can worship, the God I can relate to as a Father who inspires me to emulate his goodness and who suffers with me when evil, be it of the innocent blindness of nature or the moral blindness of man, brings affliction upon me and those I love or any of God's creatures. I would suggest that the difficulty in relating to an aloof all-powerful deity has led millions to focus their worship on gods in human forms or on Saints who appear more receptive to their needs. Is it not paradoxical for individuals to maintain that God must be totally independent of man, totally self-sufficient, totally powerful, and then on the basis of the evil in the world to deny his existence? What *is* essential is for each of us to find a God in *whom* we can believe, *who* can be our companion in life, *who* will listen to our prayers, *who* will ignite the divine sparks that reside within us, and by bringing out the best in each of us lead to the ultimate victory of good over evil.

My belief in immortality is *also* rooted in the faith that the good in man will someday be victorious. I do not deny the traditions of my Jewish heritage on this subject, but believe that the essence of the divine promise of immortality is the affirmation of the ultimate value of each human life. The Rabbis of old said that he who saves a single life saves the world and he who destroys a life destroys the world. The belief in the immortal life of the human soul should not be a sop to those who suffer in this life by the promise of something better in the World to Come. It is far better to live as though it were all happening here and now. We should seek our immortality in the effect we have on others by what we do and what we say. As the pebble thrown in a pond causes ever widening ripples, so do our actions have endless influence, which gives our lives eternal meaning. If there is an After Life where good souls bask in the light of God's presence and are reunited in spirit with those whom they loved, I would be very pleased, but I would not live my life any differently were this not so. Loving and doing kindness is its own reward.

Rev. Rōshi Jiyu-Kennett

Abbess, Shasta Abbey, The Order of Buddhist Contemplatives
(Sōtō Zen)

In the Udana Scripture the Buddha says: 'O monks, there is an Unborn, an Unchanging, an Uncreated and an Undying. If this were not so there would be no apparent freedom from birth, change, creation and death.' The Sōtō Zen Buddhist saint, Keizan Zenji, calls the above 'the Lord of the House' and, sometimes, 'the Eternal' since it is necessary to be able to describe the above in words and for no other reason.

The Lord of the House remains eternally in meditation, in eternal training; unmoved, unhasting, silent. All creatures are born, die, and are born again – none impedes the Lord's work. Like the Buddhas and Patriarchs of old, the Lord helps all and teaches at all times just by being the Lord. He, She, It is not a being and is not not a being. He has no specific gender, no specific form. He is not emptiness and He is not not emptiness. We are born here, die there, born again to joy or sorrow according as we have cleansed ourselves from our karmic impregnations – the Lord waits and waits eternally. Why? I am not a god. It is enough for me to *know* the Lord of the House, more I neither ask nor seek. The Lord of the House has no beginning and no end, no past and no future. I am not Him and He is all of me.

For centuries people have caused Buddhism to suffer under the belief that it was a way of life and not a religion. This was because they feared saying the Truth lest they set up a god to be worshipped. The Lord is not a god and He is not not a god. He is not a saviour; and if, at the moment of death, a person can embrace infinity instead of his own delusions, he is immediately united with the Lord. At all times we are free to unite with, or turn away from, the Lord. If you would know the Lord know that the means of training are thousandfold but PURE meditation must be done. Through meditation we are immediately united with the Lord; together with Him we go out into emptiness, into form and again into emptiness . . .

Baha'u'llah
Prophet, Founder of the Baha'i faith

To every discerning and illuminated heart it is evident that God, the unknowable Essence, the Divine Being, is immensely exalted beyond every human attribute, such as corporeal existence, ascent and descent, egress and regress. Far be it from His glory that human tongue should adequately recount His praise, or that human heart comprehend His fathomless mystery. He is, and hath ever been, veiled in the ancient eternity of His Essence, and will remain in His Reality everlastingly hidden from the sight of men. 'No vision taketh in Him, but He taketh in all vision; He is the Subtle, the All-Perceiving.'

The door of the knowledge of the Ancient of Days being thus closed in the face of all beings, the Source of infinite grace, according to His saying, 'His grace hath transcended all things; My grace hath encompassed them all,' hath caused those luminous Gems of Holiness to appear out of the realm of the spirit in the noble form of the human temple, and be made manifest unto all men, that they may impart unto the world the mysteries of the unchangeable Being, and tell of the subtleties of His imperishable Essence.

These Sanctified Mirrors, these Day Springs of ancient glory, are, one and all, the Exponents on earth of Him Who is the central Orb of the universe, its Essence and ultimate Purpose. From Him proceed their knowledge and power; from Him is derived their sovereignty. The beauty of their countenance is but a reflection of His image, and their revelation a sign of His deathless glory. They are the Treasuries of Divine knowledge, and the Repositories of celestial wisdom. Through them is transmitted a grace that is infinite, and by them is revealed the Light that can never fade . . . By the revelation of these Gems of Divine virtue all the names and attributes of God, such as knowledge and power, sovereignty and dominion, mercy and wisdom, glory, bounty, and grace, are made manifest.

These attributes of God are not, and have never been, vouchsafed specially unto certain Prophets, and withheld from others. Nay, all the Prophets of God, His well-favoured, His holy and chosen Messengers are, without exception, the bearers of His names, and the embodiments of His attributes. They only differ in the intensity of their revelation, and the comparative potency of their light. Bahu'u'llah

Know, thou of a truth that the soul, after its separation from the body will continue to progress until it attaineth the presence of God, in a state and condition which neither the revolution of ages and centuries, nor the changes and chances of this world, can alter. It will endure as long as the Kingdom of God, His sovereignty, His dominion and power will endure. It will manifest the signs of God and His attributes, and will reveal His loving kindness and bounty. Blessed is the soul which, at the hour of its separation from the body, is sanctified from the vain imaginings of the peoples of the world. Such a soul liveth and moveth in accordance with the Will of its Creator, and entereth the all-highest Paradise. The Maids of Heaven, inmates of the loftiest mansions, will circle around it, and the Prophets of God and His chosen ones will seek its companionship. With them that soul will freely converse, and will recount unto them that which it hath been made to endure in the path of God, the Lord of all worlds. The nature of the soul after death can never be described, nor is it meet and permissible to reveal its whole character to the eyes of men. The Prophets and Messengers of God have been sent down for the sole purpose of guiding mankind to the straight Path of Truth. The purpose underlying their revelation hath been to educate all men, that they may, at the hour of their death, ascend, in the utmost purity and sanctity and with absolute detachment, to the throne of the Most High. The light which these souls radiate is responsible for the progress of the world and the advancement of its peoples. They are like unto leaven which leaveneth the world of being, and constitute the animating force through which the arts and wonders of the world are made manifest. Through them the clouds rain their bounty upon men, and the earth bringeth forth its fruits. All things must needs have a cause, a motive power, an animating principle. These souls and symbols of detachment have provided, and will continue to provide, the supreme moving impulse in the world of being. The world beyond is as different from this world as this world is different from that of the child while still in the womb of its mother. When the soul attaineth the Presence of God, it will assume the form best befitting its immortality and is worthy of its celestial habitation. Such an existence is a contingent and not an absolute existence, inasmuch as the former is preceded by a cause, whilst the latter is independent thereof. Absolute existence is strictly confined to God, exalted be His glory. Well is it with them that apprehendeth this truth.

◆§ · §◆

We have grasped the mystery of the atom and rejected the sermon on the mount.

General Omar Bradley

Ezra Taft Benson

President, Church of Jesus Christ of Latter-day Saints

◦⧼ · ॐ◦

The word *God* is a title used in the scriptures to refer to three distinct, individual beings who, together, form the Godhead: God the Father, God the Son, and God the Spirit.

God the Father is the Father of all mankind; all mortal beings are literally His spirit offspring. He is an all-knowing, all-powerful being, who is loving, kind, merciful, gracious, and perfect in every sense. His name-title is Elohim. He has a glorified, resurrected physical body of flesh and bones. Adam, the first man on this earth, was created in His image. Man is the only creation of God that is created in His image and His likeness. The physical body of God the Father receives its life from His eternal spirit; His spirit can and does communicate with the spirit of man.

God the Son was known by His name-title Jehovah before He was born on this earth. During mortality, he received the name and title of Jesus the Christ. He was the Great I AM in His pre-earthly existence. He is the Firstborn Son of God in the spirit, and the Only Begotten Son of God in the flesh. He is the Son of Man of Holiness, one of the titles of God the Father. He is in the express image of the Father's person. He is the Saviour and Redeemer of all mankind. He atoned for the original transgression of Adam, was the first one on earth to be resurrected, and provided for the resurrection of all mankind. He atoned also for our individual sins if we repent of them and if we receive the saving ordinances of His Gospel. He will return to the earth with His glorified, resurrected body of flesh and bones at the time of His Second Coming. He then will rule as King of kings and Lord of lords, and every knee shall bow and every tongue confess that He is Jesus Christ, the Son of God.

God the Spirit is a personage of Spirit whose name-title in the scriptures has been translated as the Spirit, the Holy Spirit, and the Holy Ghost. He is a revealer of truth, and he witnesses and testifies to the divinity of both the Father and the Son. The gift of the Holy Ghost is an ordinance of the gospel of Jesus Christ that is given by the laying on of hands by one holding the proper priesthood authority. This ordinance follows the ordinance of baptism by immersion for the remission of sins. Through the cleansing power of the Holy Ghost, a person may be purified from sin, and, thus, in a spotless, sanctified condition, may return to the presence of God the Father and Jesus Christ the Son.

Each mortal human being is composed of two parts: an immortal spirit that has always existed and will always exist, and a physical body of flesh, blood, and bones. At the time of death (the end of mortal life), the spirit returns to the spirit world (consisting of two major parts: paradise and spirit prison) to await the resurrection. The physical body returns to the earth or the elements from which it was created.

All mankind, *without exception*, will be resurrected from death through the atonement of Jesus Christ. Paul taught, 'For as in Adam all die, even so in Christ shall all be made alive' (1 Corinthians 15:22). This mortal, corruptible physical body of flesh, blood, and bones then will become an immortal physical body of flesh and bones with spirit replacing blood as its life-giving fluid.

Paul taught, also, that the type of resurrected body each person will have and the place where he or she will dwell eternally depends largely upon the person's obedience to the principles of the gospel while in mortality. (See 1 Corinthians 15:35–42.)

At the time of resurrection, when the eternal spirit and the immortal resurrected body are joined together, each person becomes a living soul and will continue to live as a distinct individual forever.

God is a shower to the heart burned up with grief;
God is a sun to the face deluged with tears.
Joseph Roux

Dr Natubhai K. Shah

President, Jain Samaj Europe

The focal point of a Jain Temple is an image or images of one or more of the twenty-four Tirthankars (Prophets, also known as Jinas). The image is conventionally represented seated or standing, calm and detached, worshipped as God. God, according to Jain belief, is a perfectly happy soul with infinite capacities for activities, a pure and perfect soul without any material body, a being that cannot perish or become degenerate. Jains do not believe in God as creator and ruler, but believe that every soul has existed from eternity and from eternity souls have been emerging from the ordinary embodied worldly condition into the pure liberated condition, and will continue to do so for ever, but they will never come down from this condition of Godhood to the condition of souls in the ordinary embodied states.

For all eternity, the ordinary soul has been indulging in the false attachment and aversion to other things, ignorant of its nature, and by reason of this indulgence it is never at ease. Upon the abandonment of this attachment and aversion the soul becomes calm and tranquil and when completely free from the influence of these unnatural activities, the soul lives its natural life and becomes all knowing, permanently happy and immortal. In short it becomes God.

Jains worship images in the Temple or meditate on them, not for asking any worldly favours, but to follow their examples so that one day their own souls become liberated and purified; achieve *Moksa*, the state of permanent happiness and bliss. The Tirthankars are not the creators or the rulers. Neither do the Tirthankars answer requests or control the affairs of the world. The prayers and meditation of the devotee are directed to admiration and praise of the object of his or her devotions, and to the noble aim of emulating the Tirthankars' virtues and spiritual life. In short Jain's concept of God is that of purified, omniscient, happy, blissful, all powerful and eternal perfect being, who neither creates other things or beings, nor rewards, nor punishes.

The destiny of the soul is decided by the fine subatomic particles attracted to the soul by its action or deeds (*Karma*). Whatever we do, whatever we speak, whatever we think and whichever manner these activities are done, attract different *Karmic* particles in intensity, quality and quantity. If these *Karmic* particles are mild in character, they are dissociated from the soul by feeling sorry or asking for forgiveness. If they are strong in intensity and character, they remain attached to the soul, till they get ripened, which may happen in a short time or after thousands of years. High-intensity *Karmic* particles are removed by experiencing their effects, but low-intensity ones can be removed by austerity and living a noble life. *Karmas* are like bank balances. If they are good (merit), one enjoys their fruition till they are exhausted. If they are bad (demerit), one suffers from misery.

Jain scriptures have described different kinds of *Karmas* in detail and have explained the causes of the happiness, misery and apparent inequality of this world. If some person is doing bad deeds but is still enjoying a good life (of material wealth), it is due to fruition of good *Karmas* in past lives, but his soul is collecting demerit because of bad deeds and he will have to suffer its effect in the future. When all the *Karmas* are shed, the soul is purified and remains in its natural blissful state.

Until liberated, the destiny of living beings is constant transition from one physical body to another, a recurring cycle of birth and death and rebirth. We have all of us passed through countless lives in the past, and we face countless more lives in the future.

The Soul (*Jiva*) is the one unchanging element of a living being. It may be embodied in any of four broad categories of existence, as heavenly being, human, in animal or plant form, or as a denizen of the hells. The type of being in which the soul is reborn, the shape, form, colour, longevity, etc., of the body it occupies depends upon its *Karma*.

When we die the soul rises and occupies a body which is formed by fusion of *Pudgala* or matter particles and which grows with the help of the soul, while the corpse which is made of matter gradually disintegrates in *Pudgala*. These *Pudgala* may form the body of another soul.

In conclusion, when one dies, depending upon its *Karma*, the *Jiva* takes birth in the uterus; it may be umbilical (with a sac covering), incubatory (from an egg) or umbilical without sac covering, or it takes birth of celestial or hellish beings in special beds.

The body is formed from *Pudgala* (matter) and the longevity, the happiness or misery are experienced according to the attachment of *Karma*. It may be liberated and can attain perfection and permanent happiness and bliss by annulling the previous *Karmas* by calm and patient endurance of their effects and simultaneously warding off fresh *Karmas* by the attitude of dispassion and the contemplation of their true nature. When the soul eliminates all the *Karmas*, it achieves its final pure state, *Moksa* or *Nirvana*, the state of *Siddha*. The *Siddha* is completely detached from the affairs of the universe, abiding in a state of eternal calm, bliss and total knowledge. Numbered among the *Siddha* are the Tirthankars (whom Jains worship as Gods), who in their last worldly lives attained omniscience, taught the people the path of liberation, and finally passed to the bliss of *Moksa*.

Richard Causton

General Director, Nichiren Shoshu of the United Kingdom (The Buddhist Society for the Creation of Value)

Perhaps it sounds a strange thing to say but, for me, Buddhism has explained what God really is. To put it very simply, God is Life, that supreme vital force or creative energy which permeates the universe and, at the same time, is at the heart of every living thing including, of course, all of us human beings. God, therefore, is both within and without us, whether we know it or not and whether or not we feel we deserve such good fortune.

And this situation exists, not by 'God's grace', but by the very nature of life itself.

Thus, however bad we may feel our past has been, however many regrettable mistakes we may feel we have made, we do not have to beg this unseen power for mercy, nor need we fear the wrath of God nor wallow endlessly in guilt. Rather, we should determine above all things, to start to respect and nurture the dignity of life in all its forms. Then we will discover that life is protecting us.

Nichiren, the great Buddhist sage, who lived in 13th-century Japan and whose teachings I follow, explained this ultimate truth about life in this way:

> Life itself is the most precious of all treasures. Even the treasures of the entire universe cannot equal the value of a single human life . . . Some may have wives, children, retainers, estates, gold, silver or other treasures according to their status. Others have nothing at all. Yet whether one has wealth or not, life is still the most precious treasure. This is why the saints and sages of ancient times offered their lives to the Buddha and were themselves able to attain Buddhahood. Even common mortals can attain Buddhahood if they cherish one thing: earnest faith. In the deepest sense, earnest faith is the will to understand and live up to the spirit, not the words, of the sutras.

I believe in the Buddhist perspective of life and death – that we pass through an eternal cycle of birth, growth and decline until we enter that state of seeming lifelessness that we call death, which in fact is but a period of latency, of neither existence nor non-existence before we are born again. If you like, these are the winter seasons of our own eternal cycle of life, when, just as the sap works its way through the branches and twigs of a fruit tree in readiness to create blossoms and fruit when the time is right, we can generate and conserve life-force, the creative energy, to take on a fresh new physical form once again.

Nichiren, the great Buddhist sage, said: 'Cherries, plums, peaches and pears are each supreme as they are. I, Nichiren and those who chant "Nam-myoho-renge-kyo" can equally reveal ourselves as the True Buddha.'

We too have an innate nature and character which is unique and eternal to ourselves and which relates exactly to the unique purpose which we should fulfil in each of our living lifetimes. Buddhism has led me to find that unique purpose in this lifetime and begin to fulfil it – and it cannot be denied that to be fulfilled as a human being is the greatest joy in life. Death, then, is just an interval like a night's sleep, when having cast off an ageing or increasingly inefficient physical form, we are born again and can continue our unique function in the pattern of life as a whole.

Rev. John Johansen-Berg

Pastoral Leader, the Community for Reconciliation

I believe that God is a person and in his personality he expresses all that is good and precious in human qualities since these are derived from the Divine Being. Pre-eminently he is the God of love. Whilst power could command, God chooses to offer love freely and to seek a free response from his people. At the heart of God's creation is the fundamental law of love; this is the royal law which expresses the divine heart. When God created people he intended them to live in holiness and righteousness at peace with God and with each other. When people failed God and themselves by choosing evil and unrighteous ways, becoming hateful and violent towards each other, God condemned the sin but not the sinner. He loved his people so deeply that he chose to act to redeem them, to restore them, rather than to destroy or annihilate them.

Some will ask how we can know that this is the nature of the Godhead, how we can be sure that there is not a vindictive or cruel creator, or gods of light and darkness in perpetual conflict with each other. Looking around the world and pondering on human history some would see plenty of evidence for such views.

God has not left us in doubt or wondering about these deep and vital matters. He speaks through his messengers and prophets; he inspires truth in written words which are holy books handed down through generations. God speaks in many ways and reveals himself in many places. Through these writings and these people God shows himself to be the God who cares for those who suffer, the needy and oppressed. He not only hears their cry but also responds. He is the Father who provides, the Lord who heals, the God who liberates. Such a God inspires his people to seek a new era of justice and righteousness. Whenever people choose a way of self-sacrifice and outgoing love they express something of God. For such worshippers prayer and work become one in a religion which is of the heart and which seeks the true welfare of all living beings.

As a Christian I believe that God has spoken in a particular and special way through Jesus Christ whose teaching and ministry, whose death and resurrection express his claim to be the way, the truth and the life. Jesus himself was an inclusive rather than an exclusive teacher. It is significant that people of many faiths and none recognize the wisdom of his teaching and respond to the depth of his compassion. As notable a Hindu leader as Mahatma Gandhi was greatly moved by Jesus' death on the cross and had as his favourite hymn

> When I survey the wondrous cross
> On which the Prince of glory died,
> My richest gain I count but loss
> And pour contempt on all my pride.

Jesus was quick to inspire and respond to faith in a Samaritan, a Greek or a Roman as well as his fellow Jews. He said that those who were not against him were for him. To follow Jesus then is not to turn away from people whose nation, race or faith is other than ours, but rather to welcome them, to meet with them, to listen to them and to share with them in seeking to know God more fully and to respond to him more faithfully. In doing so we shall often learn more than we teach and receive more than we give.

When it comes to sharing what we believe about Jesus, it is sufficient to tell his story and to allow him to make his own impact. The combination of his words and actions, culminating in his supreme act of self-sacrifice and his resurrection show him as one who offers us a path of salvation, a highway into the presence of God. To ignore it would be our great loss. Jesus comes to us not with subtle philosophy, nor with a series of religious laws that, if we obey, can set us right with God. Rather he expresses the divine love in such a way that we can place our trust in him. It is important that we realize that Jesus came into the world because of the predicament into which the human race had fallen. We became and are the victims of our own choices, so often wrong choices. Jesus came to put right what we had made wrong in our relationship with God and with each other. His chosen method is significant. With all the power of the divine nature at his disposal he chose to empty himself and to take the way of self-sacrifice. In an age which worships power it seems incomprehensible that someone should choose weakness or vulnerability; in a generation for which success is so important it seems absurd to accept death on a cross. With free choice in the matter it seems contrary to accept suffering. Yet in all this Jesus gives hope to the despairing, reassurance to those who suffer and affirmation for those who give of themselves for others. Jesus reveals the nature of the divine being as ready to serve rather than dominate, heal rather than injure and forgive rather than condemn. It follows that God desires those who worship him to be encouragers and befrienders, overcoming evil with good, loving enemies, being children of light. What appears to the world something of an enigma, God on the cross, becomes then a symbol of the new dawn, the expression of hope for a suffering and bewildered world.

Biblical revelation is precious to us but spiritual experience is vital in walking the Christian way. God meets with his people. There are those intensely moving spiritual experiences which change the direction of life for those who thus hear or see God or experience his signs. It may be the burning bush on the mountain or the guiding pillar of fire in the wilderness. It may be the face of Jesus seen on a mountain top or the voice of the Lord heard in the thunder of the waters. It may be the sign of the rainbow in the sky or a dove perfectly formed by a cloud; it may be the still small voice in the quiet of our own room when we are alone with God. Such moments are not easily described or shared, but they have a depth of meaning which sustains a lifetime of faith.

It is my belief that we shall survive beyond death in a new life that is spiritual. I believe that there will be continuity between this life and the next and that we shall recognize one another even as we shall see and know God. As the love of God can transform all situations and his forgiveness knows no limits, I hope that the offer of salvation can be ultimately accepted by all human beings. However, as God has given us freedom to choose or reject him, I recognize that some may reject God in this life and the next. Such would choose their own annihilation since I believe that only that is eternal which can find its meaning and its existence in relation to God, who is the supreme expression of love, joy and peace. It follows that those who respond to God's love and his universal offer of salvation will enter his presence beyond that door which we call death and will find the peace that passes understanding, will experience the joy that overflows the cup of promise and be enfolded in the love which binds all together in perfect harmony. In such holy consummation, the name of God will be honoured and glorified.

Alan Bond

Inventor of the HOTOL Aerospaceplane RB545 engine

Your first question was about personal opinions of God. Well, it depends what you mean by 'God'. Different people, I realize, have different views as to what 'God' actually is. As I understand it, the idea of God is as both a creator of humanity and a benefactor who in some broad way controls its destiny. I cannot subscribe to any of that. The creation of the human race, I feel, is the result of three individual creations.

The first one is the creation of the Universe. The second one through a series of processes, the creation of the planet Earth. And finally the creation of life itself, eventually evolving to human beings. I believe that the creation of the Earth and the creation of life are coming under very close scientific understanding. The creation of the Universe is slightly more ambiguous but none the less is starting to become somewhat understood. Understood, that is, in such scientific terms as one can understand that type of event. Even in itself, the question of understanding has a great many difficulties at that particular level.

I don't want to go on at length about the creation of the Universe itself but let me pose to you the question which occurred to me very early in my teens: who created God or, alternatively, how was God created, because it is fairly clear from all the scientific observations that we have now made that the Universe has only been here for something like 16 thousand million years – an awfully long time but still a time which we can understand. We can measure time scales and see processes that take that sort of time.

Now either God has been around for ever before that time, before he created the Universe, in which case what was he doing the rest of the time? And secondly, he may himself have been created, in which case where did his creation come from? In the event of having to assume either a God who had been around for ever, well, I could simply say all the processes which go on within the Universe have also been around for ever and therefore I don't actually need God to explain it. In the event that God himself was created, all that I have done is remove my mystery one step further beyond. As to God the controller, who in some mysterious way influences the course of all our lives, I personally have seen absolutely no evidence of all this during my 43 years of existence.

Many people would no doubt say that I have been around with my eyes closed but I have to admit that looking at other people who do feel that they have a guiding hand in their life, I really feel that they do themselves injustice. It is quite obvious to me that, in the number of people I know who feel like that, the real guidance has come from within themselves, and all they have done is disguise that fact by the appealing to a higher order of authority.

Your second question was about the after-life – life beyond the life we have. Well, again, I have no belief in such a thing. I believe that I can understand the majority of life around me including my own in terms of rather straightforward chemistry and physics and in particular that bit of – I don't know what it comes under these days – mathematics or physics which relates to information theory. Human beings, to me, are a fascinating process but only in the sense that I see within them the chemistry and the cybernetic activity which leads to all their enormous variety and diversity of behaviour. Before long there will be within our society machines and devices, maybe some of them made of similar materials to you and me, which will behave and function almost indistinguishably from ourselves. Some of those things ultimately will behave in manners that human beings are just not capable of and their quality of life, if I can use that phrase, may be infinitely richer than that which we ourselves possess.

My feeling, therefore, is that when we die all these processes actually cease and all the knowledge and stored information of my experiences will simply be lost. There is a sense in which even already the younger versions of myself are already gone. That sense is in that certainly the atoms which constitute my body change regularly. A period of about seven years sees a complete change in all the atoms which constitute my make-up. The information which remains reasonably rigid within the framework of changing atoms, nonetheless evolves, ideas get changed, the way in which I act changes, my character slowly evolves so that due to added information and experience, this entity called Alan Bond changes over the years, so that today whilst I still see those experiences embedded in my experience at present, that earlier person now no longer exists. In a sense therefore, each subsequent day is the after-life of the day before.

Now, just to summarize, you may find the above view rather gloomy, in fact I find it very comforting. I don't have to live in mortal fear of what takes place in an after-life. At the same time, I know that what I am experiencing at the present is the only shot that I will ever get at it. It is therefore up to me to make the very best of this short slot called existence. There is, in my world, no one controlling my destiny other than myself and the people around me who I interact with. It leaves me therefore captain of this ship that I sail and it is up to me to make the very best of it.

Holding the views that I do, people in the past have asked me whether I view people with religious views as being weak. Of course the answer to that is that I certainly don't. The only thing that has ever troubled me about extreme religious views is the enormous amount of suffering and bloodshed worldwide and through the whole of time that such views have brought and to me this is a tragedy since all of this has been completely wasted effort.

His Divine Grace A. C. Bhaktivedanta Swami Prabhupāda
Founder and Spiritual Teacher of the International Society for Krishna Consciousness

God is the reservoir of all knowledge, beauty, strength, fame, renunciation and wealth. God is the reservoir of everything and therefore whatever we see in this world that is beautiful emanates from a very minute part of God's beauty. As the *Gitā* says: 'Know that all beautiful, glorious and mighty creations spring from but a spark of My splendour.' (*Bhagavad-gitā* 10.41)

Being the source of all attractive qualities, God is known as 'Krishna'. Unless God is all-attractive, how can He be God? Therefore the word 'Krishna', which means 'all-attractive', is the perfect name for God, because He is capable of attracting everyone.

God has unlimited transcendental qualities and is omnipresent, omniscient and omnipotent. Many people cannot conceive how God can be a person and retain these qualities. But God is not a limited person like you and I. He is the Supreme Personality of Godhead. His personality is not finite like ours. If God is everything, how can we reject God's transcendental personality?

Just as in the material world all fathers are persons, the ultimate father is also a person. God is the father of all species of life, not just human beings. He is the Father, material nature is the Mother and the various living beings are all children maintained by the Supreme Father. This is the basis of universal brotherhood.

God is the centre of love and since everything is God's expansion, a lover of God is a lover of everyone and His love reaches everyone.

Krishna is the ultimate shelter and therefore we should approach Him for protection or relief from distress. Since He is the source of our existence, no one can be a better friend than Krishna, nor can anyone be a better well-wisher. As our relationship with Krishna matures we may wish to offer devotional service to Him and ultimately our devotion develops into pure love of God. By understanding that Krishna is the supreme enjoyer, the supreme proprietor and the supreme friend we can gain peace in this world.

We all have a tendency towards pleasure because, by nature, God is always full of pleasure. He is the Supreme source of pleasure.

Since we all depend upon God for our existence it is our duty to please Him, and Krishna in turn pleases His devotees. If He is pleased we will all be pleased. If we pour water on the root of a tree, all the parts of the tree – the leaves, and flowers and branches – are nourished.

By engaging in devotional service to God we become happy in our loving relationship with Krishna, otherwise we are in a diseased condition of consciousness and will never be able to find happiness or satisfaction in whatever we do.

What is the difference between a living body and a dead body? The difference is that when someone dies, the spirit soul, or the living force, leaves the body. And therefore the body is called 'dead'. So, there are two things: one, this body; and the other, the living force within the body.

For example, as a child grows, he becomes a boy, the boy becomes a young man, the young man becomes an adult and the adult becomes an old man. Throughout all this time, although his body is changing from a child to an old man, he still feels himself to be the same person, with the same identity. Just see: the body is changing, but the occupier of the body, the soul, is remaining the same. So we should logically conclude that when our present body dies, we get another body. This is called transmigration of the soul.

This process of transmigration is very subtle. The spirit soul is invisible to our material eyes. It is atomic in size. After the destruction of the gross body, which is made up of the senses, blood, bone, fat and so forth, the subtle body of mind, intelligence and ego goes on working. So at the time of death, this subtle body carries the small spirit soul to another gross body. The process is just like air carrying a fragrance. Nobody can see where this rose fragrance is coming from, but we know it is being carried by the air. You cannot see how, but it is being done. Similarly the process of transmigration of the soul is very subtle. According to the condition of the mind at the time of death, the minute spirit soul enters the womb of a particular mother through the semen of the father, and then the soul develops a particular type of body given by the mother. It may be a human being, it may be a cat, a dog, or anything.

We were in different bodies before this life and because we are eternal, we keep on coming back in different bodies. That body is not guaranteed to be a human body. There are 8,400,000 difference forms of life. You may enter into any of them according to your mental condition at the time of death. What we think of at the time of death depends on how we act during our life.

If, out of ignorance, we commit sinful activities and violate nature's laws, we will be degraded to animal or plant life. Then, again, we must evolve by transmigration of the soul through various species to the human form; a process which may take millions of years. Therefore a human being must be responsible. We must take advantage of the rare opportunity of human life by understanding our relationship with God and acting accordingly in devotional service. Then we can get out of the cycle of birth and death in different forms of life.

We must first come to the spiritual platform, understanding 'I am not this body'. We can come directly to this platform by chanting the holy names of God: Hare Krishna Hare Krishna Krishna Krishna Hare Hare Hare Rama Hare Rama Rama Rama Hare Hare. If we cultivate this practice on the spiritual platform, then immediately we can realize our spiritual identity. Chanting the holy name of God is the direct means of contacting the Supreme Absolute truth. Then the process of God realization becomes successful very quickly and we can become qualified by Krishna's grace to return back home, back to Godhead to live with Krishna eternally: no more change of bodies.

Shirley MacLaine

Actress and author

When I conceptualize God I see brilliant white light and I *feel* that the light is LOVE. I perceive this 'God Love Light' as an energy which infuses each one of us human beings enabling us to create anything we want.

When I die (or make my transition to the spiritual dimension) I think I will be much more aware of this light and love. For this reason I like to view 'dying' as a birth to the God plane.

Sir George Trevelyan
Adult educationalist for spiritual knowledge
Founder of the Wrekin Trust

≈ · ≈

God, to me, simply IS LIFE in its totality. Life is God. Wherever we see life manifesting, that is God in action. The Creative Source pours itself out into the ocean of Life, Light and Thought. The whole universe is a manifestation of Living Thought and Idea. These living Ideas are truly angelic beings, strands of the Thought of God. They have precipitated themselves into form. Thus with the eye of the mind we can learn to apprehend God in every created form in nature. As Alexander Pope wrote:

> All are but parts of one stupendous whole
> Whose body Nature is and God the soul.

And again:

> Mere atoms casually together hurled
> Could ne'er produce so beautiful a world.

God is The One, the great primal Unity of the Living Universe, and since He IS all life, He is in each of us, 'closer than breathing, nearer than hands and feet'. This means that He can and does live in our thinking, in direct touch.

BE STILL AND KNOW THAT I AM GOD.

And the Cosmic Christ IS LOVE, a dynamic force of harmony now launching the great redemptive process of cleansing the polluted planet.

So your two questions are of vital significance for us all NOW, at the great turning point of entry into the Aquarian Age. This generation therefore has a supremely important role to play in the great drama of redemption. For God is on the march and the changes are now beginning. If rightly seen, this is a source of tremendous hope.

The Oneness picture, the Holistic world-view, implies that the 'I' in each of us is a droplet of the divine Ocean of Life, a spark of the Divine Fire. This droplet of God, this entity of spirit, IS life. It cannot possibly die, since God is Life and therefore inextinguishable. The soul is axiomatically immortal and eternal. It always was and always will be.

The body can be seen as the wonderfully designed temple in which this divine being can operate while living through its present life-span in the heavy density of matter. The body can of course die and be dissolved, but that only releases the eternal soul-entity back into the spirit world from which it came. Thus in our death-ridden culture we can grasp that for this being, this 'I', *there simply is no death*. Survival is axiomatic. But more important is the concept of pre-existence. You were there as a developed soul before you were born. Planet Earth can be seen as the training ground for souls in long evolution through the Fall and back to God. When released from the temporary sheath of body and sense, we shall find ourselves far more alive. This in our generation is borne out in a remarkable way by the 'Near-Death Experience', when medical skill in resuscitation recovers people from clinical death. They all describe with joy, the realm of light, life and love they have entered. All doubt or fear of death is removed.

This is not dogma calling for belief. We are invited to explore living Ideas, looking at life in the light of them. Then we shall draw to ourselves inner conviction of their truth. This is the most exciting and important generation in the long aeons of evolution. We have a supremely significant role to play in the great drama of redemption of the planet.

In Christopher Fry's words, we are called on to take:

> The longest stride of soul men ever took
> Affairs are now soul size
> The enterprise

Is exploration into God.
Where are you making for? It takes
So many thousand years to wake,
But will you wake, for pity's sake?

Dr Kessavan M. Naidoo
South African witchdoctor

❧ · ❧

From intimate association with both third and first world people
– from the totally traditional African, to pioneers in science – I
have seen many similarities in their basic feelings concerning
God and the hereafter. Perhaps in this divided world, we need to
search for such common thought, from which common agree-
ment may evolve. One would not normally recognize the
similarities which exist here, because of the vast differences
between these peoples, in their affinity with nature and their
environment, and in their means of expression. Certainly it
would not have occurred to me, had my activity and therefore my
interest not been focused largely on these two extremes –
advanced scientific speculation, and primitive traditional beliefs.

It is perhaps significant that amongst these two groups, we find
those who are least influenced by the thoughts, concepts and
dictates of other people. Amongst our scientists, and particularly
our inventors, we find fiercely individualistic minds. Many of our
primitive people, still functioning in their traditional societies,
have not yet been influenced by the thinking of the rest of the
world. Yet in these widely divergent groups of people, do we find
common thought expression:

1. A feeling that one is in this world in some sort of training,
   testing, or experimental situation.
2. That there is an interactive link between the individual of this
   life and a supernatural, non-physical intelligence of immense
   power, knowledge, and permanence. Whether evangelist,

spiritualist, faith healer or witch doctor, all accept that their powers come to them from their God. Although this image of their God differs, all have been seen to perform with their spiritual assistance, otherwise unaccountable feats. Whether a western man of God or a witch doctor, their belief in the existence of a spiritual power, and the ability to reach and be assisted by their God, is a strong common factor.

3. That this non-physical entity resides somewhere in space, but through another dimension outside our powers of observation.

4. That development on earth is progressing towards some predetermined conclusion.

5. That one must, in this world, strive to reach a higher level or plane of spiritual achievement in order to be elevated after life. Although there are many variations of this concept, all relate to the widely held view of reincarnation.

6. That each individual, either upon death or at some determined time, will be judged by how he behaved and reacted to the situations and influences which he encountered during his stay in this world.

7. Perhaps the most fundamental and universal similarity which I see in the beliefs of different people is the concept that truth is the ultimate goal for which the individual must seek. Truth is always considered immutable, and the foundation of spiritual thought and behaviour.

So, we find a similarity of belief that there is a God, who is, or relates to a supernatural intelligence which exists outside our powers of perception, but who is somehow in contact with each individual in this world. As each person attempts to identify with his God, by reacting to his own concepts of God-inspired behaviour, he will in some way be rewarded, and that truth represents the communications link with his God and the vehicle to the hereafter.

What happens to us when we die seems to have been experienced by those within my knowledge, who have technically died, but somehow returned to continue their life. Such people in both the technologically advanced and the primitive traditional cultures relate similar accounts. At death one leaves the body behind and moves through space, sometimes described as passing through darkness or a tunnel, and arrives at some brightly lit destination. One is aware of tremendous physical freedom, well being, and sudden intellectual awareness. In these related experiences, the individuals returned, to find themselves alive – usually among rather startled people. These people relate a feeling of sadness at having returned, and, for a time, strange sensations as no longer having need of food or feeling physically constrained.

This act of writing to you is causing me to think, and begin to realize the nature of the problem which we are wrestling with in southern Africa. It now occurs to me that the basic problem involved at the interface of human association between the different cultures, is the virtual absence of truth. I can now identify this as the basis of the problems which arise in the interaction and the dealings between the more advanced, and the traditional cultures. From my experience as advisor to heads of governments of the emerging nations of southern Africa, I learn that truth is absent in politics; rare in business dealings; and fragile in interpersonal relationships. On reflection, it appears that the absence of truth could be the real problem behind all the problems facing humanity today. Like a poorly backed currency, truth has undergone a process of devaluation. Truth has little value today because it is not supported and held with confidence by the people and nations of the world. If truth, as common to the basic belief of all faiths, could be appreciated and valued as the basis of human and cultural interaction, most of the world's problems could be reduced. A direct relationship would develop between an appreciating value of truth, and the improvement in human relations and the easing of world problems.

My experiences lead me to say that if I have any message to convey to you, it is that you could encourage in your book, the search for common beliefs in the religions and cultures of the world. And, further, that truth should become the basis for human understanding, interaction and cooperation in resolving our present problems in order that we may begin a long delayed journey forward for humanity – and towards God.

•◌§ · ह•

Doris Stokes (1920–1987)

Clairvoyant and author

᠅ · ᠅

Medium Doris Stokes had no fear of death. When she was in her thirties she suffered an ectopic pregnancy and doctors warned her husband that there was no hope. But Doris survived to recall an extraordinary experience. In her first book, *Voices In My Ear*, she described what happened:

I opened my eyes slightly and the bed was surrounded by a beautiful turquoise light. Blue light I vaguely remembered, the healing power. I looked again and my father and my son John Michael (who passed over when he was a baby) were standing at the foot of the bed. They were smiling at me and I tried to smile back. If I'm going to die, I thought, all I have to do is go to them. Then the blue light started spinning and other colours whirled into it and I felt myself drawn feet first into a brilliant rainbow spiral. I was rushing down, my father and John Michael a little ahead of me, and beyond them at the end of that tunnel of madly flashing colours was a bright light so bright I couldn't look at it. Instinctively I knew that if I reached that light I would have passed over. Yet the only emotion I felt was relief. I don't have to fight any more I thought, it's out of my hands.

Suddenly there was a tremendous jolt and I crashed back to the bed again. The tunnel, my father and John Michael were gone . . .

. . . I nearly died but strange as it may sound, I'm not sorry. I'd been hearing about, reading about and telling people about what happens when we die and now I'd had personal experience of at least the early stages. I knew there was nothing to fear . . .

from *Voices In My Ear*, Macdonald, 1985

Margo Williams
Clairaudient and author

◆§ · §◆

My concept of God is Light, a vast Light far more brilliant than we could ever imagine or words could ever describe. A Light that is full of spiritual love. As I was born with psychic talents I have experienced many wonders such as seeing the aura of all human beings and animals, hearing the voices of earthbound souls trapped by their own guilt and finding their lost artefacts by digging for them and thus releasing these unhappy spirits, and seeing visions which often have deep religious meanings. Usually a small silver light appears on the ground where an article lies buried or surrounds a vision. I believe there is a little of this Holy Light within us all and it is up to us as individuals as to how we use it. Some use it wisely while others smother it and so often turn to crime. The earthbound who I have released, in many cases spoke of continuing their journey through a tunnel towards the light and that is how I see God – a never-ending powerful loving Light.

I believe when we die we go through a passage towards a light, leaving our earthly body behind and, upon reaching it, the soul rests for a period; we are then judged according to the way we have lived. Some who have completed their earthly cycles go to the next plane to learn more and in time go to the Light, becoming part of the Godhead; while others, who have not yet experienced all types of lives and opportunities given, or who have not completed their tasks on earth, or by the selfish way they have lived, are sent back, reincarnating many times to fulfil their work or put right wrongs from previous lives. Some, however, may return by choice as they feel they have a vocation to help others. I believe, however long it may take, all souls reach the Light and become one with God.

Kwok Man-Ho

Chinese astrologer and author, International Consultancy on
Religion, Education and Culture

There are many different gods in popular Chinese Buddhism;
the number may vary according to the person you talk to but
many believers, like myself, have their own favourite deity.

In Hong Kong and Tai Wan, Kuan Yin, the goddess of Mercy,
is particularly popular. She is my personal concept of God. She
answers every prayer, from the wealthy and poor alike, in
whatever way she thinks appropriate.

The fishermen and sailors of China and Hong Kong are
especially devoted to her and shrines and monasteries to her
honour can be found on boats or near ports. She is a goddess for
the people and I know that during the recent forty years of
religious suppression in China, Kuan Yin was the goddess
secretly worshipped and prayed to in homes throughout that
country. Now that restrictions have been lifted and the public are
free to sacrifice and worship there are many stories of her
supernatural powers told by monks, nuns and laypeople.

Although we are unable to see the gods it doesn't mean they
are not with us. There are spirits around us wherever we go and
whatever we do. Several years ago when I was visiting Hong
Kong for a holiday, I climbed Lion Rock hill. Just as I was
approaching the summit I slipped on a stony path and began to
roll towards a steep cliff face. I knew my life was in danger. Again
and again I called out to Kuan Yin and I suddenly felt her power
alongside me; a moment later my fall was broken by a tree, the
only tree on the edge of that cliff face.

Another time I collapsed from a severe stomach rupture and
was taken to hospital. I had extensive internal bleeding and I
knew that my life was threatened. At one moment my mind was
clouded, my body numbed by loss of blood and I heard the doctor
urging the nurses to rush me to casualty. Once again, I prayed to
Kuan Yin with all my heart and the next moment I became calm

as Kuan Yin appeared clearly before my eyes. I believe it was a miracle for I recovered in several days without needing an operation.

She is the goddess who rescued me and will always be with me. I have a small shrine to her in my house and each day I burn joss-sticks before her and offer prayer. Her birthday on the 19th day of the 2nd month in the lunar calendar is particularly important to me, as is the celebration for the day she became a Buddha, the 16th day of the 6th month in the lunar calendar.

As a Buddhist I believe that our conduct in previous lives produces an effect in this life. Our rebirths may be in one of the following six forms: as Buddha, Immortal, human, hungry ghost, beast or in hell. Our bodies are temporary and our soul only abides there for a lifetime before passing on to another place. Our body is the means by which our soul provides service to others. At death our soul may go to heaven as an Immortal or a Buddha, it could return to earth to pass another human life, it may be left to wander painfully as a hungry ghost or beast or it could be condemned to the suffering of hell. Our actions may have escaped judgement by the police but they will not escape judgement by the gods. I believe that this is why some people are bestowed with good fortune but others are born into poverty and pain. But good fortune in this life is not a free licence to harm others with destructive thought or action just as bad fortune should not prevent kind thought or action. Whatever merit we accumulate will be passed on to our next rebirth and whatever wrongdoing we have committed will be punished accordingly.

As the bird alights on the bough, then plunges into the air again, so the thoughts of God pause but for a moment in any form.
Ralph Waldo Emerson

Dr Max Ferdinand Perutz CH, CBE

Molecular Biologist, Nobel Prize for Chemistry 1962

⋅

I do not believe in God or any life after death, but we should live as if God existed and follow Christ's teaching in order to be in harmony with the world and with ourselves.

Janet and Stewart Farrar

Pagan witches

⋅

We have been practising white witches, running our own coven, for seventeen years now. Twentieth-century Wicca is a new phenomenon rooted in very ancient foundations. It is a pagan religion. That is to say, it is very much Nature-based, acknowledging and endeavouring to fulfil our responsibility to, and integration with, Mother Earth, her rhythms, and her creatures. It is not dualistic; that is to say, it does not regard matter and spirit as being in conflict with each other, as 'evil' and 'good', but sees both as valid and interactive elements in the total spectrum of Divine manifestation.

It acknowledges the one ultimate Divinity, but may approach it through many God (and Goddess) forms.

We worship the same Divinity as anyone else, because granted that a divine creative principle exists, there can only be One. (The idea that witches worship Satan is a hangover from the deliberately engineered hysteria of the persecution centuries.) We simply personify It in a way which helps us to attune ourselves to It – as every religion does.

The Ultimate is unknowable at our present stage of development. 'My face ye cannot see', except maybe in rare incommunicable glimpses. We cannot comprehend or relate to It until It starts to manifest; and there can be no manifestation without polarization. That is why we worship the God and the Goddess.

For us, these two concepts are the primal creative polarization of the divine Ultimate. They personify the high cosmic Activity which all lesser activity, all the manifested universe including ourselves, all the levels of reality from spiritual to mental to physical, inevitably reflect.

A simple metaphor for this is the electric battery. Without its two terminals, which are equal and complementary, no current flows. The God and Goddess are the terminals of our cosmic divine battery. The God-aspect represents the energising, fertilizing, linear-logical, analyzing polarity. The Goddess-aspect represents the formative, nourishing, intuitive-cyclical, synthesizing polarity. To these two concepts we find we can relate religiously, intellectually, and in day-to-day living. They enable our own current to flow. Two millennia and more of patriarchy have attempted to banish the Goddess aspect altogether, to the great spiritual impoverishment of human thinking.

Witches use many God and Goddess forms, not because we believe these forms are separate divine entities, but as a way of appealing directly to an appropriate 'face' of the God or Goddess. We recognize that the Ultimate has an infinity of wavelengths, for which many different but appropriate tuning-signals may be used.

To us, there is no 'great gulf fixed' between the divine and the human. We see the universe, on all its levels of reality, as a vast organism. The Ultimate, as manifested in the God and the Goddess, is its life force, its intelligent creative principle. But men and women, and all creatures animate or supposedly inanimate, are like cells in that organism. Mother Earth can be called the limb or organ of that organism of which we are most immediately a part; she depends on our healthy functioning, and we on hers. We are an integral part both of the limb, and of the total organism.

Mother Earth is not only a limb of the cosmic organism. She is also our most vivid face of the Goddess; She gives birth to us, nourishes us, dazzles us with Her beauty, awes us with Her inexorability, and sets our feet dancing to Her rhythms. Open our eyes and our souls to Her, and it is impossible not to love Her. And for a woman, there is an instinctive identification with Her; for just as every cell carries the chromosomes of the total organism, so every woman is of the essence of the Goddess, and every man of the God.

As for Him – perhaps the most evocative and best-loved pagan God form is the Horned God of Nature: a Pan-like figure, embracing the whole range of the male polarity, the God-essence, from His earthy goat-feet through His fertilizing loins to His intelligent, music-making head. A man who is himself whole can identify with Him, and a woman respond to Him.

Nor should we forget that other magical element in our environment, which has haunted mankind's imagination since the dawn of time: the Moon. She is the perfect symbol of another Goddess-aspect – the intuitive gift which casts a clear but gentle light on the treasures of the Unconscious. She is the cyclical Dark Lady of Secrets, who rules the tides of the Earth and of life; and every woman can identify with Her if only through the monthly rhythm of her own body.

In case it should appear that all this implies too rigid a division between Goddess and woman on the one hand, and God and man on the other – it must always be remembered that each contains the seed of the other. If we open ourselves to them, Goddess may speak directly to woman, and God to man, by identification; but they also whisper constantly to the other half, by resonance with that buried inner seed.

Our relationship to God and Goddess, and thus to the Ultimate of which They are the first expression, is magical, spontaneous, undictated by dogma; we attune ourselves to Them through the living symbols with which They have been wise enough to surround us.

Almost universally, witches believe in reincarnation. This is the accepted belief of a probable majority of those in the world who credit survival after death in any form; and it was taught in the early Church, as St Jerome and St Gregory testify. Its basic tenet is that each individual soul experiences life after life on Earth, learning its lessons and perfecting itself until it is ready to progress to a higher stage of harmony with its Creator. This belief depends on the theory of multi-level reality – as do all religions in one form or another, though occult (including Wiccan) thinking tends to define the levels more subtly than most.

A generally-accepted pattern of the levels would be:

SPIRITUAL: The ultimate essence, divided into the Upper Spiritual, or Divine Spark, and the Lower or Concrete Spiritual.
MENTAL: The plane of intellectual processes and concepts, also divided into Upper and Lower.
ASTRAL: The plane of emotions and images, also divided into Upper and Lower.
ETHERIC: The tenuous, near-physical energy web which links the Physical to the other levels. It is intimately involved with the aura which sensitives see – and, it can be argued, with the phenomena recorded by Kirlian photography.
PHYSICAL: Material manifestation.

The Spiritual and Upper Mental levels are the immortal part, generally known as the Individuality. The Individuality is her-maphroditic, containing the qualities of both genders. The remaining levels – the Personality – belong to one incarnation only, being built anew each time, and either male or female.

On physical death, the human entity abandons its physical body and the etheric link associated with it. The entity now consists of the Individuality plus the Lower Mental and the Astral levels of the Personality, and is thus still emotionally identified with the incarnation which has just ended. He or she lives for a while on an astral/mental plane often called the Summerlands.

Here he or she associates with others who are at the same stage, including people known during the recent incarnation. The nature of this stage, and one's reaction to it, depend very much on the level of development which one's reincarnating self has achieved.

Finally the Individuality sheds the remaining elements of the Personality, and withdraws into itself, to absorb and learn from the experience of its last incarnation. When this withdrawal period is over, the Individuality starts to acquire the 'outer shells' of a new Personality (which may be male or female), culminating in physical birth to a new incarnation.

Two other concepts should be mentioned. One is Karma, a Hindu word which has been adopted because there is no exact English equivalent. It means, so to speak, the spiritual bank balance, the debit or credit of one's actions, which is carried from life to life and must sooner or later be completely balanced. The other is that individuals may be drawn together in life after life, by the pull of Karma, whether negative or positive.

What do we find are the spiritual and emotional effects of belief in reincarnation?

First, we find it much more plausible and 'fair' than the theory of single Earthly lives, of varying brevity, culminating in one-off verdicts of eternal bliss or eternal torment. A Creator who knows we must develop at a believable pace is much easier to respect and love.

The knowledge that the life we are living at present is not the whole book, but merely one of many chapters, encourages a healthier sense of proportion. Remembering the workings of Karma, we know on the one hand that we can never permanently get away with wrongdoing, and on the other that apparently undeserved suffering cannot remain permanently uncompensated.

With the best will in the world, if one believes that the Earth is only a fleeting incident in the eternity of one's existence, then it is like a hotel room. One may enjoy it, and try to leave it tidy and undamaged for later occupants; but one cannot really identify with it.

But to us, Earth is home; it has been home for many lives past, is now, and will be for an unknown number of lives still to come. Everything about it is our continuing responsibility and invites our love. It is here that we must work out our spiritual advancement.

For as Jesus pointed out – the Kingdom of Heaven is not 'up there', in some other environment. It is within us. Where we are.

It were well to die if there be gods,
and sad to live if there be none.
Marcus Antoninus

Jonathon Porritt
Director, Friends of the Earth

My God, first and foremost, is a weaver of rainbows, a regretful, rueful deity, horrified at the ruination of the flood, and keen to make amends with a somewhat sodden Noah:

> 'And behold, I establish my covenant with you, and with your seed after you, and with every living creature that is with you, of the fowl, of the cattle, and of every beast of the Earth with you. I do set my bow in the cloud, and it shall be for a token of a covenant between me and the Earth.'

To humankind fell the not unreasonable task of acting as steward of God's Earth, a task of which we have made so comprehensively botched a job that the more fatalistic amongst us might justifiably be awaiting the second deluge rather than the second coming. To be a true servant of God today, one must surely be a warrior of that rainbow covenant 'with every living creature'.

Sadly, religion has made of itself too fine and abstracted a thing to accept the natural world as the primary revelation of the divine to most men and women. We no longer know how to sing the song of the Earth; there is concrete between, and technological superabundance, and the discord of distorted reason. We are no longer at home in our earthly home. In the words of Archbishop William Temple: 'The treatment of the Earth by man the exploiter is not only imprudent, it is sacrilegious. We are not likely to correct our hideous mistakes in this realm unless we recover the mystical sense of our oneness with nature. Many people think this is fantastic. I think it is fundamental to our sanity.'

In order to be at home in the world, we must be fully of it, experiencing it directly as mud between our toes, as the rough bark on a tree, as the song of the world awakening every morning.

The Earth speaks to something in each and every person, even when we are imprisoned by concrete and steel. In that dialogue lies a form of celebration as primitively powerful as anything to be found in our anaemic, emaciated culture.

> To see a world in a grain of sand,
> And a heaven in a wild flower,
> Hold infinity in the palm of your hand
> And eternity in an hour.

William Blake was right to make no mystery about this. To relate to the Earth in this way is natural, ordinary and theoretically accessible to everybody. The spiritual can and often should be utterly mundane. The problem is that fewer and fewer people have access to the Earth in that way, either because they are imprisoned in their urban hell, or bound by the equally demonic constraints of conventional education, religion or politics.

Ultimately, therefore, my God is inevitably and passionately political, *of* the Earth and all its people, not above it. Stripped of the spiritual dimension, politics in today's world is a hollow shell; religion stripped of its political dimension is irresponsibly escapist. There would be no ecological crisis if people lived by the words of Christ, or truly comprehended the implication of Gandhi's dictum that 'the world has enough for everyone's needs, but not enough for their greed'.

And so, as a militant friend of God's Earth, with a highly developed penchant for pantheism, I can only declare my allegiance to the rainbow, that most fleeting of physical phenomena, yet most enduring of metaphysical 'tokens'. You can keep your pot of gold that's meant to be at the end of it; I seek only the ability to sing again the song of the Earth.

Birth and death are for me wholly earth-bound processes, for I have never been able to *imagine* life after death or to get particularly worked up about it. Indeed the pre-occupation with 'the life to come' rather than with 'life here and now' has clearly been part of the philosophical baggage used to condone humankind's laying waste the Earth. 'Dust to dust and ashes to ashes' is just about the most environmentally aware statement in the Christian faith! The prospect of being nibbled away by worms may be aesthetically disturbing, but it's enormously satisfying from an ecological point of view. Death is but the closing of one cycle of life and the opening of another.

The Bishop of New York
The Rt Rev. Paul Moore Jr

I think of God as a mystery of being beyond space and time and within the infinitesimal reaches of the universe; the mystery of being behind what we cannot understand by reason – birth, death, love, suffering, beauty. I believe that we can communicate with that mystery of being through prayer, both in the literal sense of the word, as well as through leading prayerful lives. I believe we sense a presence of the mystery of being in the love we have one for another, in the struggle for justice and the sacramental and worshipping life of the Church and all the kinds of love – friendship, romantic love, sexual love, love between parents and children, married love, a love for those in need. I believe within the mystery of being there is a creative power which brought the universe into being and continues to sustain it. The redeeming power which we came to know in Jesus Christ, through his teaching and through his life, his death, and the mystery of his Resurrection, and through the spiritual power by which we sense the presence of the mystery of being within our lives. In the traditional language of the Church, we refer to this as the Holy Trinity – one God, one mystery with three ways of being and three ways by which we come to know that mystery.

That part of the mystery of being to whom I relate most constantly in prayer and daily life is Jesus Christ. The spiritual experience which means the most to me – day in and day out, year in and year out – is the Holy Eucharist.

I do not know what will happen to me when I die, but I believe that God is merciful and forgiving, and I believe the human person is of ultimate importance and will somehow continue in a state of being after what we call death. What that state of being will be like is beyond my comprehension, but I trust it will be a time of peace and love and joy. Even using the word 'time' is not right because we are speaking of eternity.

The Fourteenth Dalai Lama
His Holiness Tenzin Gyatso

As Buddhists we do not believe in God as a creator. In fact Buddhists do not believe in the concept God as in Christianity or Islam. Secondly, the Buddhists believe in the theory of rebirth – to be reborn, not necessarily in the human form, but in the countless forms among sentient beings.

TIBETAN VIEWS ON DYING

How we die, the process of dying and how to prepare for it:

Death, being unwanted, has been analyzed since the distant past both within and outside of religion. In Buddhism, the first of Buddha's teachings is that of the four noble truths, and from among the four truths, the first is that of true sufferings. It is important to recognize suffering. There are three types: the suffering of pain itself, the suffering of change, and the pervasive suffering of being under the influence of a contaminated process of conditioning. After you recognize suffering, you need to identify its causes and get rid of those causes. It is necessary to cultivate the path consciousnesses by which you achieve the cessation that is the extinguishment of the causes bringing about suffering. These are the four truths: sufferings, the sources of suffering, the cessation of suffering and its causes, and the paths that bring about such cessation.

The four truths are divided into sixteen attributes, four for each truth. The four attributes of true sufferings are impermanence, suffering, emptiness, and selflessness. Within the topic of impermanence, there are two types – coarse impermanence and subtle impermanence. Subtle impermanence refers to something that scientists who take an interest in minute particles can describe because they are not just taking for granted the appearance of a solid object such as a table, which seems to be the one that was here yesterday, but look at the changes within the smaller elements that compose objects. The substances which compose these external objects disintegrate moment by moment; similarly, the internal consciousnesses which observe those external objects also disintegrate moment by moment. This momentary disintegration is subtle impermanence. Coarse impermanence is, for instance, the destruction of an object, or in terms of people, it is a person's death.

There are great benefits to being mindful of death. If suffering is recognized, its causes can be researched, and, above all, it can be faced, confronted. Sooner or later death will come. We do not want it, but once we are under the influence of contaminated actions and afflictive emotions, it will definitely come. If right from the beginning you think about death and prepare fully, such preparation can help when death actually comes. This is the purpose of becoming mindful of death.

How? If you believe just in this life and do not accept its continuation, it does not matter much whether you are mindful of death or not. Meditation on death and impermanence is based on the theory of the continuation of a consciousness in rebirth. Once there is another lifetime – a continuation of consciousness in rebirth – it can only be helpful to prepare for death since, if prepared, you will most likely not be anxious and frightened by the process of dying, nor complicating the situation with your own thought.

If there are future lifetimes, the quality of the next lifetime depends upon this lifetime. If you conduct your life now in a good manner, this will be beneficial to the next one. Anger, attachment, and so forth cause us not to conduct our lives in a favourable manner, leading to harmful results in the future, and a cause of generating these unfavourable states of mind is the conception of permanence. There are other causes such as the conception of the inherent existence of objects, but when you are able now to decrease the degree of the conception of permanence, attachment to this lifetime becomes weaker. Also, when you are able to keep impermanence in mind – seeing that the very nature of things is that they disintegrate – most likely you will not be greatly shocked by death when it actually comes.

To overcome death entirely, it is necessary to end your own afflictive emotions. For, by overcoming the afflictive emotions, birth ceases, and thus death ceases also. To do this, it is necessary to make effort, and to generate that exertion it helps to reflect on death and impermanence. From thinking on death and impermanence, you generate an attitude of not wanting such, this in turn drawing you into investigating techniques for overcoming death.

Also, through reflecting on death and impermanence, your concern solely with superficial matters limited in scope just to this lifetime will diminish in strength. Death will definitely come. If you spend your life overly concerned with just the temporary affairs of this lifetime, and make no preparation for it, then on the day when it comes you will be unable to think about anything except your own mental suffering and fear and will have no opportunity to practise anything else. This can produce a sense of regret. However, if you have reflected frequently on death and impermanence, you know that such will come, and you will make preparation at an easy pace with plenty of time. Then when death actually comes, it will be easier. Still, I have heard from a few hospital workers that some who have no concern about a future life die more easily than some religious persons who worry about the next lifetime.

Since the mind at the time of dying is a proximate cause of the continuation into the next lifetime, it is important to use the mind near the time of death in practice. No matter what has happened in terms of good and bad within this particular lifetime, what happens right around the time of death is particularly powerful. Therefore, it is important to learn about the process of dying and prepare for it.

Within the Bodhisattva Vehicle and specifically in the Mantra [or Tantra] Vehicle, there are explanations that correlate the three types of bodies – Truth Body, Complete Enjoyment Body, and Emanation Body – that a Buddha has in the effect stage with three types of processes that we naturally have in the ordinary state – death, intermediate state, and rebirth. Three paths are presented by which these ordinary factors, which correspond in rough form to enlightenment factors, can be used. In these explanations which are unique to Highest Yoga Mantra, it is also said that knowledge of the process of dying is extremely important.

In terms of how to prepare for death, in Buddhism there are explanations found in sūtra and mantra, and within mantra, explanations according to the three lower tantras – Action, Performance, and Yoga Tantra – as well as according to Highest Yoga Tantra. What is the entity or nature of death? It is the finishing or ending of life. In Vasubandhu's *Treasury of Knowledge (Abhidharmakosha, Chos mngon pa'i mdzod)*, life is said to serve as a basis of warmth and consciousness, whereby death is the ending of that function. Thus, while this temporary, coarse body and consciousness are together, one is alive, and when they separate, that is death. It is necessary to distinguish between coarse, subtle, and very subtle body and mind; death is the separation of consciousness from the coarse body as there is no way for the most subtle consciousness to separate from the most subtle physical level, the latter being just the wind or inner energy on which that consciousness is mounted.

Different conditions of dying are described. One is to die when the lifespan has been exhausted; another, to die when your merit has been exhausted; and the third is to die in an accident. The latter would be a case, for instance, of drinking, getting drunk, driving, and killing yourself on the highway.

A vague indication appears near the time of death as to what kind of rebirth you will be taking. This is seen in how the warmth gathers within the body. For some people the warmth begins gathering, or withdrawing, from the upper part of the body, and for others it starts to withdraw first from the bottom part. It is worse for the warmth to start gathering from the top down and better for it to gather from the bottom up.

Some people die peacefully; others die within great fright. To the person who is dying, various appearances, pleasant and unpleasant, dawn to the mind.

In terms of explaining the process of death from the point of view of the mantric system, in Highest Yoga Tantra death is explained as the cessation of coarse winds or energies. Since death is related with the cessation of inner energies and these inner energies depend upon the body, a knowledge of the structure of the body is important. In the mantric system, the topics that are mainly explained here are those of the channels, inner winds, and drops of essential fluid. In the sūtra system, eighty thousand channels are set forth whereas in the mantric system there are seventy-two thousand. From among these, three are most important – the central channel running from the forehead to the top of the head and down to the base of the spine with channels on its right and left sides. In terms of the internal winds or energies, many different types are explained, but ten are most important – five main and five secondary winds. The essential drops are the red and white constituents. In general, beings die similarly in the sense that the process is culminated by the dawning of the clear light of death; however, due to various types of coursings in the channels by these inner winds and drops, different types of appearances occur to a dying person. Also, because of minor physical differences the process differs slightly from person to person.

In the stages of dying, twenty-five factors are said to dissolve. These are called the twenty-five gross objects:

Five aggregates:
  forms, feelings, discriminations, compositional factors, and consciousnesses
Four constituents:
  the four elements of earth, water, fire and wind
Six sources:
  the eye sense, ear sense, nose sense, tongue sense, body sense, and mental sense
Five objects:
  visible forms, sounds, odours, tastes, and tangible objects
Five ordinary wisdoms:
  basic mirror-like wisdom, basic wisdom of equality, basic wisdom of analysis, basic wisdom of achieving activities, and basic wisdom of the nature of phenomena.

During the actual process of dying, these factors dissolve in stages. Marking these stages are different external physical signs as well as internal signs. For these signs to occur gradually and in order, the constituents of the dying person must not have been overly consumed by disease, and the person must not have died suddenly in an accident. If you die in an accident on the highway, these eight stages will dawn quickly, and you will not have a chance to practise anything, suffering the double loss of accidental death before your time and of not having a chance to practise in conjunction with the gradual unfolding of the stages of dissolution. If you die naturally, the signs will appear gradually in order.

The first stage is represented by the dissolution of the aggregate of forms. In rough terms, when the aggregate of forms begins to disintegrate, this means that the earth constituent is losing its force in the sense of becoming less capable of serving as a basis of consciousness. Simultaneous with this, the capacity of the water constituent in your body to serve as a basis of consciousness becomes more manifest; this process is called 'dissolution of the earth constituent into the water constituent'. As an external sign of this, your limbs become thinner, more frail, and the freshness of your appearance deteriorates. You have the sense that your body is sinking under the ground, and your eyesight becomes unclear.

At this time, the internal sign, according to the *Guhyasamāja Tantra*, is that you have a visual sense of seeing a mirage. However, according to the *Kālachakra Tantra*, you have a visionary sense of smoke. This variance in explanation arises from slight differences in the physical structure of the channels, winds, and drops of essential fluid in the respective trainees of those tantras, specifically in the number of channel petals at the channel wheels at the top of the head and at the throat, for instance. Both of these tantras describe six channel centres in extensive form and four in brief form but differ with respect to the number of channel petals.

After that, in the second stage, the aggregate of feelings dissolves. At that time, the water constituent decreases in force in terms of its capacity to act as a basis of consciousness, due to which that capacity of the fire constituent [the factor of heat in the body] becomes more manifest. As external signs, the fluids of the body dry – your mouth dries, the fluid in the eyes dries a little, and your eyes move less. According to the *Guhyasamāja Tantra*, internally, the sign of this stage is that you have a sense of seeing an appearance of smoke.

In the third stage the aggregate of discriminations dissolves, at which time the fire constituent lessens in force in the sense that it is less able to serve as a basis of consciousness, the wind constituent thereby becoming manifest in terms of this capacity. As an external sign, your sense of heat diminishes, the heat of your body having become withdrawn; in terms of your own thought, your memory of the affairs of close persons deteriorates. As an internal sign you have a sense of an appearance of fireflies or scattering sparks.

In the fourth stage the aggregate of compositional factors dissolves, at which time the capacity of the wind constituent to act as a basis of consciousness weakens. As an external sign, your breath ceases. As an internal sign, you have a sense of a burning reddish glow from a flame; previously there were many appearances like fireflies and so forth, which become more and more subtle, leaving just a reddish glow. In general, people consider this to be death because your heart is no longer beating and you are no longer breathing. If a doctor came, he would say you were already dead; however, from our point of view, you are still in the process of dying; you have not yet died. Your sense consciousnesses have disappeared, but the mental consciousness remains. However, this does not mean that you could revive.

Within the mental consciousness there are many levels of coarseness and subtlety. In Buddhist texts there are assertions of different numbers of consciousnesses – nine, eight, six, and one – although the most prevalent assertion is of six consciousnesses. The Mind Only School Following Scripture asserts eight – the five sense consciousnesses, the mental consciousness, an afflicted mentality, and a mind-basis-of-all. The latter two terms are also used in other contexts with different meanings; thus, the usage of those terms does not necessarily involve an assertion of eight consciousnesses in accordance with this Mind Only School.

Beyond mere number, consciousness can also be divided into main minds and mental factors, the former being the mere knower of the entity of an object and the latter being that which differentiates the features of that object. The general character of consciousness is mere luminosity and knowing, which pervades all consciousnesses. Its entity is mere luminosity, unobstructed by anything; its function is to know based on the appearance of whatsoever object.

In the production of a visual sense consciousness, for instance, three conditions are needed – an empowering condition which is a physical sense faculty; an observed-object-condition which here is a visible form, a colour or shape; and an immediately preceding condition, a former moment of consciousness. When these three are complete, a consciousness apprehending a visible form is produced. The three conditions have different functions; the fact that the consciousness is an entity of luminosity and knowing is due to the immediately preceding condition; that it apprehends visible form and not sound is due to the empowering condition, the eye sense faculty; that it is generated in the image of a colour or shape is due to the observed-object-condition, the object itself. This is how a coarse consciousness is produced.

Here, however, during the process of dying the bases of these coarse sense consciousnesses – the eye sense faculty, ear sense faculty, and so forth – have deteriorated, on account of which the consciousnesses associated with them cease. Still, there are four levels of grossness and subtlety within the minds that remain, and thus there are four further stages of dissolution of the elements. The coarser begin to dissolve first, starting with the eighty conceptual thoughts. These eighty conceptions are divided into three groups, respectively characterizing the next three subtler levels of mind. Thirty-three have the nature of the mind of radiant white appearance; forty have the nature of the mind of radiant red increase; and seven have the nature of the mind of radiant black near-attainment. The level of fluctuation – great, middling, and small – of the inner wind or energy that is the mount of these three groups of conceptions serves to illustrate the nature of the movement of the wind or energy associated with the three subtler levels of mind.

When the eighty conceptual thoughts together with the winds or energies that serve as their mounts dissolve, the internal sign is that a white appearance dawns; this is the mind of radiant white appearance. It is compared to a clear autumn sky filled with just moonlight. There are no more external signs.

When the mind of radiant white appearance dissolves together with the wind or energy that serves as its mount, a more subtle mind appears, this one being called the mind of radiant red increase. It is compared to a clear autumn sky filled with just reddish or orange sunlight.

When the mind of radiant red increase dissolves along with its mount, a still more subtle mind appears, this being the mind of radiant black near-attainment. It is compared to the complete darkness of a clear autumn sky in the first period of the night. During the initial part of this level of mind, you are still aware, but then the capacity for conscious awareness deteriorates, and you become as if unconscious.

When the mind of radiant black near-attainment dissolves together with the wind that serves as its mount, the most subtle of all minds appears – the clear light of death, actual death. It is compared to an immaculate dawn sky in autumn, without any other appearance. The mind of clear light is called the fundamental mind because it is the root of all minds; in relation to it, all other minds are just adventitious. It is this mind that exists beginninglessly and continuously in each individual through each lifetime and into Buddhahood. An explanation of this is given only in Highest Yoga Mantra.

During the phases of dissolution, it is important to be aware; as much as you are aware, so much greater is the capacity to remember the previous life after rebirth. This is like the fact that if at night before going to sleep we strongly determine with clear awareness what time we want to rise in the morning and what we are going to do after rising, then even if while asleep we are not remembering this, due to the previous intentionality we rise right at that time and immediately remember what we are to do. In the same way, during these phases of dying, as long as awareness remains, you should take care to maintain its capacity in full alertness.

A person who dies naturally within physical well-being and without much physical deterioration will remain in the state of this subtlest mind, the mind of clear light, for about three days. During this time the subtlest consciousness still resides in the old body. Some exceptional people, who through practice during their lifetime have been able to identify the nature of mind and have engaged in practices concerned with the channels, winds, and drops, are able to recognize the process of death such that the clear light dawns within maintaining full awareness. Due to their control, they can remain in this state for a week or even a month according to their own wish. About ten instances of this have occurred among Tibetans since our arrival in India in 1959.

Even in the hot season in India people have remained in the clear light for two weeks like someone asleep – no longer breathing, like a corpse but, unlike a corpse, not smelling.

When within that subtle mind of clear light there is a very slight movement, the mind of clear light ceases, the consciousness exits from the old body, and you begin the reverse process, going back into the mind of radiant black near-attainment and the other six levels of appearance – radiant red increase, radiant white appearance, appearance like a burning butter lamp, appearance like fireflies, appearance like smoke, and appearance like a mirage. If you are to be reborn in the Desire Realm or Form Realm – a rebirth requiring an intermediate state (*antarābhava, bar do*) – at the time of the mind of black near-attainment the intermediate state begins. If you are to be reborn in the Formless Realm, there is no intermediate state.

For those who pass through an intermediate state, it ends with the connection to the new life state, at which time you pass again through the eight signs of death culminating in the dawning of the mind of clear light of death. If you are taking rebirth in a womb, the connection to the new life in the mother's womb and the dawning of the mind of black near-attainment after the clear light of the death of the intermediate state are simultaneous; thus, in a certain sense, a life begins with the mind of clear light.

Generally speaking, the ordinary life state is involved in the grossest level of consciousness; death, in the subtlest level; and the intermediate state, in a middle level. Similarly, within the twenty-four-hour period of a day, the ordinary waking state is on the grossest level of consciousness; deep sleep, the subtlest level; and the dream state, in an intermediate level. Again, when a person faints, the mind becomes more subtle. Thus, in an ordinary day we pass through these various levels of mind though not in the full manner of the process of dying.

In conclusion, it is very important to identify your own basic mind, the mind of clear light. To realize the subtlest mind, the first step is realization of the nature of mind on the conventional level. With realization of the nature of mind you can concentrate on mind itself, gradually increasing the power of realization of the entity of consciousness. Through that method, the mind can be controlled. The strength of control, in turn, helps to stop coarse minds, and once those are stopped, subtler minds will automatically manifest. If, before death, you can realize the subtle mind, this subtle mind can be transformed into wisdom – the strongest weapon to destroy ignorance and the suffering it induces. For a practitioner there is much to be learned and much training to be done.

from *Kindness, Clarity and Insight*, Snow Lion Publications, 1984

Spike Milligan
Comedian and author

A LIFE AFTER DEATH STORY FOR CHILDREN

Once upon a time there were two butterflies, with green, gold and red wings, they were called Mr and Mrs Lovely. One day Mrs Lovely laid two little white butterfly eggs under a leaf, so the rain wouldn't give them a cold. After a few days the eggs hatched and out came two brown and yellow spotted hairy caterpillars; they looked around. One was called Ding, and the other was called Dong; when they stood together they were Ding-Dong.

Ding said: 'I'm so happy being a caterpillar.'

'So am I,' said Dong. 'We are both young, and we are going to have a lovely time eating nice green leaves, playing caterpillar games, and lying in the sun and sleeping in the moon.'

They had a super time, sometimes birds tried to eat them, but no! Ding and Dong looked all smellypoo – and the birds didn't want to. Ding and Dong used to eat a hundred leaves a day! They were very happy, but one day, they both started to feel very strange; they got all sleepy and they didn't feel happy anymore. Their friend, a big black beetle called Tiggle Toggle said, 'I think you are both going to die!'

'Oh dear,' said Ding.

'Oh Ding,' said Dong.

'What happens when we die?' said Ding.

'Well,' said the black beetle called Tiggle Toggle, 'some people say you go to heaven.'

'What's heaven like?' said Ding and Dong.

'I don't know,' said Tiggle Toggle. 'People say it's a place where God lives and when you die you go there and he makes you happy.'

'We don't want to die,' said Ding and Dong. 'We're *already* happy.'

Then a deep voice said, 'There's no such place as heaven.'

They looked up and there was a big black vulture called Lumpy-Conk. 'When you die that's the end of you,' he said and flapped his wings.

Poor Ding and Dong cried – the next week Ding and Dong fell asleep, and slowly they turned into dirty brown cocoons. They stopped moving and became very still.

'Yes, they're dead,' said Lumpy-Conk. 'I'm going to eat them all up.'

But Tiggle Toggle the beetle said, 'Don't you dare! If you do I'll bang you on the beak with a conk-hammer.'

This frightened off Lumpy-Conk who flew away to his nest to play his banjo.

All winter the two little cocoons of Ding and Dong lay still, stuck to the leaves and everybody said, 'Poor things, they haven't moved for over a year, they must be dead.' And everybody forgot all about them except Tiggle Toggle the beetle, who came once a month and put little forget-me-not flowers by the bodies. But, one sunny day, Tiggle Toggle was walking along a branch to put flowers on Ding and Dong when he saw something *magic* happening!

The two little coffins of Ding and Dong split open . . . and out came two beautiful butterflies, scarlet and green and purple.

'Whoopee!' said Ding and Dong. 'Look at us! We're not dead anymore,' and they flew up and down the garden drinking honey from the flowers and playing aeroplanes.

'Tiggle Toggle was right,' said Ding. 'This is better than being a hairy caterpillar.'

Tiggle Toggle the beetle was right, there *is* a heaven, and they flew through the summer gardens with thousands and thousands of coloured flowers.

Acknowledgements
❦ · ❧

We would like to thank first of all the many people who have contributed so generously towards *My God* for without them this book would simply not exist.

We would also like to thank Mukunda Goswāmī and Akhandadhī dās for their support and suggestions; Peter Newby for putting us in touch with the right people; Pelham Books, our publishers, with whom it has been a great pleasure to work; Anne McDermid of Curtis Brown for all her help; Peter Mahon for getting the ball rolling in the first place and special thanks also to Susan Nollet our secretary.